PAPER DINOSAURS
"Rich" The New Dirty Word

Edward V. Mirabella

DEDICATION

Paper Dinosaurs is dedicated to the hard working and highly productive individuals that have spent their careers in Commercial Banking. No amount of government criticism can take away the feeling of accomplishment that comes from helping a business grow and prosper.

CONTENTS

INTRODUCTION

The young professionals that are either embarking on or considering a career in Commercial Banking should be aware of the evolution that has taken place in this industry during the past fifty years. While much of the criticism and condemnation launched by our government has been warranted, it has in my estimation gone much too far, and maligned a proud profession. What you are about to read, is an anthology of one person who spent an entire career in commercial banking. Learn from it, and profit from the mistakes of the past as you move forward.

PROLOGUE

No industry group has received more negative press than the American Banking System since the Financial Meltdown of 2008. I watch look and listen to a never ending litany of criticism from the media, consumer groups and our government. Much of this criticism is warranted of course. The repeal of Glass Steagall is often identified as a primary cause of the renaissance in financial services that may well have resulted in a total collapse of the banking system as we knew it. The expansion of financial services after Glass Steagall was encouraged by the same politicians that are now attempting to over regulate the banking industry which has made banking as I knew it, a thing of the past.

The Federal Government stepped in and passed new regulations to safeguard the system, closed or merged thousands of institutions bailed out others and levied huge fines against them. Our government also took every opportunity to define this entire industry as "tools of the rich". Many elections were won promising to right wrongs and ensure that it could not and would not happen again. Under the TARP the Federal Government took equity positions in those banks that were in the deepest of trouble, and forced other banks to accept TARP money regardless of the fact that they were in sound financial condition. You hear very little about the windfall profits that were generated as the banking industry became healthy again, when those shares were sold back into the market at a huge profit. I guess its ok for the government to generate profits in exchange for taking on great risk. Not so for business.

Recently the government at the State and Federal level has decided that they haven't done enough to this industry and are now looking to generate more financial penalties through Civil & Criminal actions. I guess they are looking to close their own budget deficits by going after the private sector again. It amazes me that we the voters only recourse towards elected officials who renege on promises, overspend and initiate lousy legislation is to vote them out of office. If they were held to the same standards that they have created for business we would have far fewer politicians because many of them would be incarcerated, or at the very least would be fined.

The Banks or to use another synonym, "the rich" have been portrayed as the enemy. This is an industry that employs millions of hard working Middle Class people who have been cast into the new definition of the banking industry. The new catchphrase "too big to fail" has been bantered around by government officials that are part of a bureaucracy that has certainly become "too big" and has constantly failed. Maybe it's time for the voters to consider breaking up the government and indict those elected officials that have brought significant damage to our country and its economy.

A majority of our elected officials have never spent a single day in private business but they profess to know what is right for us. The banking & business communities should look within its own ranks for electable candidates and begin the long process of turning things around. This process would also require banks and businesses to educate their employees and their customers about the negative and counterproductive results of regulation that has stalled our growth and hindered the creation of new jobs. The best defense is a good offense. We must stop reacting and start acting.

As a veteran of the banking industry, an individual who worked hard for over forty three years, I think it's time to tell another story. It begins in 1963 when a young sailor was released from the U.S. Navy for hardship reasons. He went back to Brooklyn, New York and accepted an entry level position at Bankers Trust Company. His generation also saw massive changes to the industry. Rapid expansion combined with a constant array of new services that ultimately enabled these institutions to create new jobs and hire people to fill them. Some mistakes were made in my era also.

Capitalism in its' true sense does work. Increased control by government has only resulted in a constant fear of criticism, and a reluctance to do what banks are supposed to do. Lend money and take risks. Remove the risk factor and many icons of business that we take for granted would not be around today. Try applauding the successes and stop magnifying the mistakes that were mostly made with the best of intentions. Our politicians should easily understand that last statement.

Hopefully the aforementioned statements will not result in an IRS audit. Read on my friends, about simpler times.

CHAPTER ONE

The Trailways Bus pulled out of the terminal in Norfolk Virginia for the long ride home. I was dressed in my Navy whites, and was seated by a window looking out at the dingy row houses that lined the streets just outside the Naval Station. I was headed back to Brooklyn where the future was uncertain at best. I reflected on the last 24 hours as the bus rolled onto the highway.

I had been seated at my desk in the supply office on the USS Forrestal when I was summoned to the Commanding Officers quarters. It was a Sunday night and the ship was leaving for the Mediterranean the following morning. This was an unusual occurrence for any sailor and I made my way to the Captains cabin as quickly as possible. My gut told me, that something was wrong. I didn't have to wait too long to find out what it was. I was told to take a seat in the captains' office and wait for his arrival. Within seconds he came through the cabin door and told me that he had received a call from my uncle regarding a family emergency back in New York. My father was seriously ill and my mother who is totally deaf needed my support immediately. He showed real concern and compassion for me as he spoke. My uncle had stressed that Mom was totally deaf and that I was an only child. No siblings to help out.

The Red Cross had been contacted to process the request, and formally submit it to Naval Operations. He explained that situations like this were usually handled quickly, but without approval I would be leaving with the ship the following morning. He told me to pack a bag anyway and wait for his call, when and if he heard from Naval Operations. I thanked him for his help and headed back to my quarters to pack. I called home and spoke with my uncle. My dad had suffered a major stroke caused by an Aneurism deep within his brain. I didn't fully understand the serious implications of his illness, but I did understand the need for me to get back home as soon as possible. I packed a bag for the trip home, took a hot shower and decided to get some rest for what could be a long day ahead.

I climbed into my bunk and tried to sleep without much success. Thoughts of an early discharge from active duty for humanitarian reasons bothered me immensely. I had joined the Naval Reserve in February of 1961, at the age of 18, after one semester at NYC Community College, and counted the days until I would be required to begin active duty. I desperately needed to get away from home and joining the Navy seemed like the only option I had at the time. I would be free of a domineering mother, and would certainly accept the military structure that I would have to adhere to as the lesser of two evils. Mom became totally deaf at the age of sixteen after a bout of Diphtheria that was contracted when he was thirteen. The hearing loss was so gradual that she began compensating for it by reading lips until a teacher recognized that she was missing much of the classroom lessons if he was facing the blackboard instead of the class.

This "act of God" as it was termed by the various doctors that were sought out for possible treatment, left her with an uncanny ability to read lips without any formal training. Since her hearing loss occurred in her teens she had normal speech. She would learn over the years to strongly rely on others to assist if a person did not move their lips when speaking. That reliance fell on me as a very young child when I would communicate for her when necessary. Now I would have to return to that life and I wasn't happy about it.

I felt a deep sense of guilt because I didn't want to go home. I liked the Navy life and had seen a big part of the world during my first year on active duty. I had toured most of the Mediterranean with stops in Italy, France, Spain and Portugal. I wasted those days in waterfront bars talking with barmaids named Brandy, Princess, etc. and bought them expensive drinks that looked like Kool Aid. I promised myself that I would do things differently on my next "Med Cruise".

I awoke to the sounds of Reveille coming from the large speakers mounted in the corner of each compartment, and immediately felt the massive ship moving. I dressed quickly and ran up the ladders to the hangar bay of the aircraft carrier to see the Norfolk shoreline disappear. We were headed out to sea and the anticipated phone call had not been received. "I guess I will see Europe again". That thought was short lived. The loud speakers blared, "Seaman Mirabella, grab your gear and get to the flight deck immediately". The next half hour was a blur. I raced below deck grabbed my duffel bag and made my way to the flight deck. A Navy helicopter was waiting for my arrival. I climbed aboard and watched the ship disappear in the distance as the chopper headed back to Norfolk. The pilot told me that the Navy had agreed to grant me emergency leave, and I would in all probability be discharged from active duty after processing at the Brooklyn Navy Yard. When the chopper landed I was given a one way bus ticket back to Brooklyn and a ride to the bus terminal.

The eight hour ride went by quickly. The bus was filled with sailors either going home on leave, or going home for good. The mood was light and the conversation always focused on the last port that they stopped at, or their plans for life after the US Navy. I guess I should channel my thoughts to helping out at home and planning my own future outside the military. "It is what it is". Why didn't Mom and Dad have more children? An only child is often perceived as a spoiled brat, but that was never the case with me. I was born to a handicapped mother and was relied upon to help her communicate with the world from the time when I was old enough to talk. Joining the Navy was my escape from that life. Circumstance had dictated that I return to it. I had no choice but to deal with it.

When the bus finally pulled into the terminal in Manhattan, the sailors dispersed in every direction and I took the subway back to Brooklyn. I arrived at the house around ten at night on Monday June 13th, 1963. I found my uncle sitting in the kitchen with my mother. He was trying to calm her fears regarding my dads' prognosis for recovery. I joined them at the table and mostly listened until he left for home about an hour later. Mom wanted to talk, so I listened until I felt my eyes starting to close. Time to get some sleep in my own bed.

I reported to the Brooklyn Navy Yard the next morning for processing, and was told to return on Friday. I spent the next few days with Mom, talking to doctors, who determined that Dad would never be able to return to work. The stroke had not taken away his ability to walk or talk, but the metal clip that was surgically implanted around the Carotid Artery to stem the flow of blood to the Aneurism in his brain was only a temporary fix, and he might live somewhat normally for a few years before he suffered another stroke that might end his life. If it were only that simple! What we were about to face was another 14 years of strokes, surgeries, hospitals & nursing homes until he finally passed away. Mom and Dad would certainly need my support in many ways during those years and I would do my best not to disappoint them.

On Friday June 18th, 1963 I returned to the Navy Yard and met with Lt. E. B. Glover to review the terms of the "hardship separation" from active duty that the US Navy had granted. I was handed a typed form, #DD214 to review and sign. I remember reading one line over and over. It referred to a hardship separation "at the convenience of the government". What the hell was that supposed to mean? Would I still be on the ship in the Mediterranean if the government decided it was inconvenient to discharge me? Who decides on the issue of just what is convenient or inconvenient for the government? What are the parameters? Did the Navy have to replace me immediately with another sailor who could use a typewriter or wield a pencil? I guess I was important to the Navy after all, and I appreciated the fact that they weighed all aspects before granting me permission to go home and help my family.

Now the Navy was faced with the important task of finding another sailor to fill my slot on an aircraft carrier whose only mission is to get the planes in the air in time of war. The ship and its crew are totally expendable. Launch those jets laden with bombs before the enemy sinks the ship and its' crew. I came very close to seeing what war is all about during the Cuban Missile Crisis. I guess dealing with Mom won't be so bad after all.

I returned home late Friday afternoon with the thoughts of what I would need to do the following week. Dads' car was sitting at the curb in front of our house. I knew how to drive but I didn't have a license. Everyday we would visit him at the hospital several times, stop at the supermarket on the way home, and we used mass transit in all of our travels. I would go to the Motor Vehicle Department on Monday morning to start the process, and hoped that it could be accomplished quickly. I no sooner opened the front door when Mom advised me of a job interview that she had arranged for me the following Tuesday. It was at a Bank.

"Mom, I just got home from the Navy. I have a million things to do next week before I can even think about getting a job". I don't want to work for a bank. I always wanted to be a rock and roll singer or a porn star, but I didn't have the voice or the equipment for either of those fields. Maybe I'll take the test for the Police Department or some other Civil Service position. Good benefits and retirement. "No way, I am not going to work at a bank". Her reply was simple and to the point. "Oh yes you are", along with the standard clichés about living under her roof etc. Fighting with her was never a wise choice, and under the present circumstances I decided it was best to abide by her wishes.

After dinner I turned on the 6 o'clock news and caught a news clip of a young reporter standing outside the gates of Sing Sing prison. He was waiting for the release of the notorious bank robber Willie Sutton who had served time for multiple offenses. As Sutton walked out of the prison gates a free man, the reporter called out to him and asked. "Hey Willie, why did you rob those banks"? The reply was immediate. "That's where the money is kid".

Maybe I'll go for that interview on Tuesday......

The weekend went by quickly with trips to the hospital, along with all the side trips to the supermarket, the butcher, the local delicatessen etc. When we got back to the house I was expected to make all those necessary phone calls to provide an update on dads' condition. Mom was always needy and controlling, and she seemed to really enjoy having me to boss around now that dad was no longer available to fill that role. She constantly reminded me of her handicap, and how she expected me to be there through these trying times. That was nothing new to me, as I had been listening to those same words since I was old enough to walk and talk. I did understand and had made a conscious decision to see her through these trying times.

On Monday morning I took the bus to the Motor Vehicle Department to start the process that would ultimately get me a drivers' license. I waited in line for about an hour and when it was my turn I walked up to the window that said "information" and started to tell the clerk my story. I needed to get a license as quickly as possible because......I never got to finish the sentence because the clerk shoved some blank forms toward me, and told me to fill them out and then proceed to the next line. I complied and went to the next window. While the clerk was reviewing the completed forms I rambled on about my fathers' illness, my mothers' handicap, me being the only child, and how important it was to be able to drive legally as soon as possible. This clerk had also been well trained in appearing to "not give a shit", as has been my experience with government agencies throughout my life, when I realized that I had started to cry from frustration. I was totally embarrassed and tried to wipe the tears away before anyone noticed. Too late. The clerk looked at me for a few seconds and said; "take a seat over there along that wall and don't move until I come to get you".

Within five minutes she came looking for me and said, "Follow me". She handed me the completed documents and ushered me into a small room that contained a table and a few chairs. She administered the written test for a learners permit, and three hours later I took the road test in dads' car. I can still envision the large rubber stamp with the words "Interim License" as it left its image on my learners permit. I had managed to find the one person in that vast government office that was willing to bend the rules and regs, to help someone in need. I guess wearing my Navy uniform was a good idea after all. I drove back home with the radio blaring and a Marlboro hanging out of my mouth. It was cool to smoke in those days.

When I walked into the house Mom was ironing my one suit. She had already washed and ironed my only white shirt, and gave me one of dads' best ties to wear for my interview the next morning. With everything going on I had completely forgotten about it. She always took great pride in her appearance, and that trait spilled over with me. For most of my 19 years I was told to put on clean underwear and socks "without holes in them" before you leave this house. She didn't want to be embarrassed if I was hit by a car and taken to the hospital. What would they think of a mother who let her son go out dressed like that? It never entered her mind that I might be killed and probably crap my pants as a result. The doctors would surely take notice of the dead boy with his big toe sticking out of his sock and record that fact on the death certificate, along with the other disgusting details that accompanied my demise.

Mom was an overachiever because of her handicap, and always demanded the same from me. It took many years for me to understand the reasoning behind it. If I was imperfect it would always be traced back to her being totally deaf.

CHAPTER TWO

The next morning I dressed, ate some breakfast and allowed Mom to look me over and nod her approval. I walked to the subway station and took the train into Manhattan and got off at the Wall Street station. I climbed the subway stairs out onto Wall Street. It was a warm sunny morning as I looked for the headquarters of Bankers Trust Company. I immediately saw the towering building with the golden pyramid which adorned the top of what I considered to be a skyscraper in those days. I walked towards the building and hoped that it was air conditioned. I wasn't used to wearing a suit and tie, and wondered how people did it on a daily basis, especially in the summer. The lobby was cool and I smiled.

I was approached almost immediately by an armed security guard. His uniform was dark blue, wrapped around a starched white shirt and necktie; brass buttons down the front of his uniform jacket, and his shoes were highly polished in the military tradition. He must have had a military background. I could never figure out the need for "spit shined shoes" during my stint in the Navy, during the routine working day. Shined shoes were in my opinion, for dress uniforms or parades. Working on board the ship could be dirty at times and my shoes would get dusty. Late at night I would re-shine those shoes, and "yes" I would spit on the rag to bring them to a glossy luster, only to return to work the next day and get them dirty all over again. The Navy would hold an inspection before work each day. The Duty Officer would walk slowly down each row of sailors and reprimand anyone who wasn't dressed to military standards, right down to his shoes. Made me feel that Mom wrote those rules.

"Can I help you young man?" Yes sir, I have an appointment with Mr. Potterfield in Personnel. "Please follow me." He took me to a bank of elevators and told me to get off on the ninth floor. "The receptionist will direct you from there. Fifty years later, in the current environment I would be asked to sign in down in the lobby, provide some form of identification, wait while security called the individual that was expecting me, and finally wear a clip-on access card complete with a tracking chip, before I was put on that elevator. This little comparison of "then & now" serves to set stage for my sojourn into a banking career that spanned 43 years.

Mr. Potterfield's office featured a large mahogany desk complete with a felt blotter, pen and pencil holders which appeared to be brass, a small lamp and a phone. I also noticed a Rolodex. For those of you that are too young to know what that is, I will explain. Long before computers and cell phones the Rolodex was used to store names, addresses and phone numbers of coworkers and business associates on individual 3 by 5 inch index cards that were arranged alphabetically. There were no fax numbers, email addresses or alternate cell phone numbers; just basic information. If you tried to call someone and got a busy signal, you kept on trying the number until you got through. If you ultimately gave up, you might dictate a letter to your secretary. Today's young banking executives never encountered a secretary taking shorthand, who then typed it on a typewriter using carbon paper to make extra copies. It would be mailed out at the end of the day and hopefully the person who received it would call you. Defining short hand, dictation and typewriter could add another chapter to this book, so I'll just move on. As I perused the big oak desk I took particular notice of the bronze name plate that sat directly in front of me as I stood next to a large leather side chair.

Mr. Potterfield stood and extended his hand for the traditional handshake and directed me to have a seat in that chair. There was no offer of coffee or bottled water back then. Any small talk was indeed "small" and the interview began. He asked questions and I answered then to the best of my ability. He inquired about the most basic skills that related to use of an adding machine and a typewriter. I assured him that I was proficient in the use of both as a result of working in the supply office while in the Navy. I also knew how to answer the phone in a professional manner, place a call on "hold" when necessary and direct the call to the proper individual. I was asked to account for the time period which began after graduation from Erasmus Hall High School in Brooklyn in June of 1960, and when I reported for active duty in the Navy, in May of 1962. My reply was immediate. I worked several part time jobs and attended college for two semesters.

Mom had reminded me repeatedly to mention that I had a year of college before entering the Navy, and will return to school at nights now that I've been discharged. In those days very few had college degrees and those that did came from wealthy families or were awarded scholarships based upon scholastic achievement. I can assure you that I wasn't included in either category. I was just an average kid that did enough to get by and graduate. My Dad was a factory laborer that never made more than a hundred dollars a week in his entire working life, and Mom was a seamstress for the neighborhood women in an effort to make a few extra dollars.

Mr. Potterfield showed genuine interest in my plans to return to school and the pragmatic interview evolved into a conversation. He mentioned a training program that would enable an entry level employee to move up quickly and possibly become an officer of the bank in a little as seven to ten years. That would be an eternity in this era. The fact that I had some college under my belt made a difference. Most entry level employees stayed in the same job for their entire career, with little opportunity for advancement. I would of course have to perform at a high level and continue my education with tuition assistance from the bank after one year of service. I wasn't just being offered a job. I was being offered a career opportunity. I felt myself relax, conversation came easily and then the unthinkable happened.

The leather chair farted.

I was leaning forward to hand a copy of my college transcript to Mr. Potterfield when it happened. The train ride into Manhattan had been hot and humid. No air conditioned subway cars in those days. I could feel the perspiration in the collar of my shirt and the back of my slacks were damp and sticky. As I slid forward on the chair the combination of sweat dampened material and soft leather produced an impressive sound that I would have been proud of if the venue was different. I found myself blurting out, "that was the chair sir, not me". He never looked up from his desk. He simply said, "That happens more often than I'd like to admit". Should I have said anything at all? Ignoring the sound might have been interpreted as a sign of guilt. I could have invited him to walk around the desk to determine that there was no foul smell. Then it hit me. "Thou dost protest too much". I let the conversation return to the original theme.

The remainder of the interview circled around a short term training program which lasted a week and then some time spent as a floater back in Brooklyn until a permanent position became available in one of the many branch offices. All future training would be "on the job". I found my thoughts gravitating to the known fact that banks closed at 3PM, and I would be home early each day. I would be proven wrong in the very near future. What a customer of a bank perceived or assumed was very different from reality, and I would learn not to assume anything over the next 43 years.

Now it was time to move on in the interview process and meet with Jim Clifford who ran Metropolitan Banking at Bankers Trust Company. "Do you have the time to do that today Ed"? I answered yes immediately, thanked Mr. Potterfield for his time and navigated my way to Mr. Clifford's' office.

Metropolitan Banking was the administrative arm of the expanding branch system in an era when banks were forced to reach out to the consumer and small business community through an ever expanding branch system. That practice would continue for decades until the banking industry started to evolve through technological developments. With rare exception, all banking services emanated from the branch locations, and the convenience offered by the local bank was a prerequisite to growth and profitability. Mr. Clifford's staff supported more than one hundred branch locations in their need for personnel, salary administration, branch security, cash deliveries etc.

As additional services were launched, training and implementation of those new services became another task for the Met Banking staff. Over time the sheer size of the support staff that was necessary undermined the ability to operate profitably. There was little efficiency in banking in that era. Tons of paper changes hands every day. We were referred to as pencil pushers, and the biggest technological advance came in the form of a typewriter that would allow a person to type a document and use carbon paper to make extra copies. Hence the term "Paper Dinosaurs". In 1963 it was however the only way to function.

CHAPTER THREE

Jim Clifford's office was much larger than that of Potterfield, and was lavishly furnished. He sat behind a large mahogany desk flanked by two side chairs. A small couch occupied one wall, complete with a coffee table in front of it and two more chairs to accommodate informal conversations. Several lamps adorned the end tables on each side of the couch and the wall above it was adorned by several proclamations, awards and his college degree. Access to his office was guarded by his personal secretary. She worked for no one else but him, and probably had little to do during much of the workday because Mr. Clifford attended frequent meetings and enjoyed lengthy lunches that started at noon and lasted several hours at a minimum. The role of the private secretary would change immensely during the next two decades and all but disappear by the nineteen nineties. It was now eleven fifteen and the interview process moved at a fast pace.

Clifford was a husky Irishman with a ruddy complexion and was impeccably dressed. He smiled throughout our chat and told me that I would be used as a floater after my week of training until a permanent assignment opened up. I nodded my approval and made a comment regarding my ability to float on my own as a result of my stint in the Navy. He looked at me and smiled. Then it apparently hit him that I had made a joke, and he chuckled and said "that's funny". The last thing he said to me before I was handed over to a subordinate for one last interview stuck with me throughout my banking career. "Ed, you come into work every day, do a good days work, don't get caught stealing and you will have a job until you retire. You will however never get rich working for a bank." He was right.

He was preaching job security and at that stage of my life, it was good enough for me. In 1963 loyalty was expected regardless of how poorly you were paid or how poorly you were treated. It was unthinkable that an employee would move from one bank to another for any reason. If your skill set was needed you might be hired by a competing bank, but you would never be fully accepted there because your loyalty was suspect. Within five years that philosophy would change in an increasingly competitive market.

He wished me good luck, shook my hand and ushered me to a much smaller office occupied by Tom McDermott. Within ten minutes he was finished with his speech of encouragement, looked at his watch and escorted me back to personnel for further instructions. I was told to return to 16 Wall Street the following Monday to begin my training. Was this last interview even necessary? He was intent on getting rid of me as quickly as possible and mumbled something about a lunch date.

It would be many years before I understood how things are done when an individual is accommodated with an interview as a direct result of a referral. It's irrelevant as to whether or not an offer of employment is made. It is however very important that the referral source not be embarrassed. Mom would certainly report the day's events to the person who reached out to Bankers Trust on my behalf. That person would conclude that Maes' son had received a fair shot at obtaining employment, and he was hired.

On the train ride back to Brooklyn I loosened my tie, opened the top button of my starched white shirt and thought about the interview process that I had just participated in. My starting salary would be $90.00 a week. That was an annualized salary of $4680.00 a year. I was twenty years old and living at home. I found myself calculating my weekly expenses, clothing that I would need to purchase, some additional money for the weekend and savings each week to complete my ultimate goal of buying my own car. Mom would have her own ideas about my personal finances. I would fight her on this issue and she would prevail again. It would be a few years before I appreciated her non- negotiable position on financial matters.

When I returned home she was sitting on the front steps waiting for me. One look at my face and she knew that I got the job. It was one o'clock and I was hungry. We talked about the interview over lunch and she decided that we would take the train to Klein's Department Store first thing in the morning. We had to be there before the doors opened to get the best buys. This was their semiannual sale when everything was marked down. I had joined her one other time for this event and it wasn't funny or pretty, but I did need a wardrobe that was suitable for a bank employee.

There I was early the next morning standing in a crowd of hundreds of women who were talking, laughing and joking while they waited for the security guard to unlock the doors. That mood underwent a radical change when the first door was unlocked. Women were pushing, shoving and cursing to get through the doors first. Some fell and were stepped over by others. Mom held my arm until the initial wave subsided and we walked in together. She made a quick right turn towards the stairs that led to the basement. The crowd had disbursed throughout the store and when we reached the men's clothing department we were alone.

Mom rushed through the racks of suits and grabbed two in my size. She pushed them into my arms and walked quickly to the shirt display. Here there was nothing to think about as she scooped up a half dozen in white, fourteen inch neck and thirty two inch sleeves. In 1963 white was the industry rule for shirts. A few neckties later and we were on line to pay for the items .I had received some "mustering out pay" from the Navy and took out my wallet to pay for the new clothes. Mom insisted on paying for everything and I didn't fight with her. She muttered something about my first paycheck but I wasn't paying attention. I was too busy watching the mob of shoppers that was still filing into the store.

As we were leaving the store at 9:30 AM I understood the reason for urgency. Get there early, grab what you need and get out. The store was now packed with bargain hunters and the men's wear area was hectic. A woman would attempt to pull a suit off the rack and someone else would grab it out of her hands. It was pandemonium, but worth it. I now had an initial wardrobe that would get me through the first year at the bank. An hour later back at home I was standing on a chair wearing the new suit pants and jacket while Mom pinned the cuffs, adjusted the waist and fitted the jacket. When she was done, those inexpensive suits and two dollar shirts looked to be custom made. This was nothing new to me as she had done it so many times throughout my life. She could take a Robert Hall suit apart and give it a custom look in a matter of hours, complete with hand stitched lapels. I took it for granted back then. I'm amazed by it now.

After dinner that night Mom wanted to talk about my first paycheck and had some suggestions on how I might budget my expenses from payday to payday. I told her that I had it all figured out down to the last penny. She proceeded to ask me if I had included "room and board" in that budget. I looked at her for a long moment, then at Dad and then back at her. She went on to explain that I would now be expected to contribute to the household expenses and starting on my first payday she wanted ten dollars a week. I couldn't believe my ears. "You don't need my money Mom". Dad looked at her and said one word. "Mae"! Her reply was the standard one. "You shut up. If he can live somewhere else for forty dollars a month including rent, utilities, food, laundry, let him do it. Case closed". I knew better than to argue so I signed onto the program.

I was paid every two weeks in those days, and I would place twenty dollars on the kitchen counter on alternate Fridays. She never said thank you, because she didn't think she had to. She was entitled to that money and I thought she was being mercenary and cheap each time I paid her. Several years later when I was planning to buy an engagement ring Mom took me to the jewelry district on Canal Street to look for a suitable ring. I started to sweat when she pointed to a ring that cost several thousand dollars. I didn't have anywhere near that amount. She took me aside and opened her pocketbook. "See that bankbook on the bottom of my bag"? "Yeah, so what"? "Take it out and open it. Look at it". I opened it and read the names across the front page. Amelia Mirabella in trust for Edward V. Mirabella.

"You do have the money to pay for that ring. This is your money. I've taken something from you every time you got paid since you were eleven years old and had that newspaper route. I deposited every penny in this account. You didn't like it, but I knew that someday you would understand why I did it". The balance read two thousand three hundred and eighty four dollars and twelve cents. She went on to explain that she didn't trust me to save as a kid, so she decided to save for me. "Happy I did it son"? I kissed her on the cheek. I learned a valuable lesson that day. Many years later I would apply the strategy to one of my own children.

CHAPTER FOUR

The following Monday morning I reported to 16 Wall Street for processing which took an hour. All the payroll forms were completed along with the various tax forms and I was ushered into a small training room. I was joined by two men who were going to provide me with Branch Banking Basic Training. They both had smirks on their faces as they spoke and saw humor in everything they said. I wanted to ask them why they joked constantly and laughed at everything, but thought better of it.

The first day I was tested on a variety of subjects including math, spelling and typing. I found it boring but tried to appear interested. The rest of the week I learned how to use a variety of adding machines, check writers, and the much feared NCR machine, which posted transactions and interest payments on savings accounts. The sheer size of the machine frightened me. This was the new technology in 1963. Many customers still walked into the bank each day holding a small black book. The teller would record the day's transaction in that little book manually and initial it. Savings accounts were a relatively new service for a Commercial Bank like Bankers Trust. Even the customers would define the institution as a business bank. The list of services was small. Business checking accounts,

Regular checking accounts that were restricted in their use to only the most important customers for their personal banking needs, and loans. There was always a huge vault in each branch that also housed the Safe Deposit Boxes. That's where cash was buried or hidden from the tax man.

These were simpler times when all services were provided by the local branch. The personnel in those branches also had the authority to make decisions and yes, approve loans. Anyone who has worked in the industry has been introduced to the five "C's" of credit at some point in their career. They are; Capacity, Collateral, Capital, Character and Conditions. While all five are prerequisites in making a decision to grant or deny a loan request, two of them would ultimately determine the final decision when dealing with the local merchants that banked at a particular branch. They were Character and Capacity. These two categories would deal with an individuals' business ethics and the depth of his pockets if the loan went bad. I'll discuss this area in greater detail later on.

I finished my training that Friday and was told to report to the branch location in Bensonhurst on Monday morning. I would be needed in the General Cage because the Note Teller had gone on vacation for two weeks. Ok, what the hell is a General Cage and who the hell is a Note Teller? Those two grinning, giggling idiots had forgotten to "train" me on that subject matter. No matter, I'd get the answers soon enough. I had a more pressing matter to deal with.

I was working in an age before computers, and couldn't simply go to Map Quest for directions and time needed to get there from my home in Flatbush. The New York City Transit system didn't have a toll free number back then either. I had to rely on relatives, neighbors and friends for directions. What bus or train or combination of both would get me within walking distance of the branch? Most of their replies started with the words, "I think", which didn't serve to build my confidence in their advice. Ultimately I got aboard a bus that headed in the general direction and asked the driver to guide me. He also began his reply with the words, "I think".

On Monday morning I put on one of those new suits, a white shirt and tie. Mom smiled her approval as I walked out the door. "Do you have exact change for the bus? I nodded yes and walked to the corner bus stop. I gave myself two hours travel time and was standing outside the huge brass doors of the bank at seven thirty, a full hour before anyone was expected to open the doors. Banks were open to the public from nine through three, leading to my assumption that I would be done for the day at three. I would discover that my reasoning was incorrect before that first day was over.

Since I had an hour to kill, I would have coffee at that little luncheonette across the street. I ordered a cup and bought a newspaper to pass the time. There were several men sitting at the counter with me, also dressed in suits and ties. The man behind the counter brought me my coffee and asked if I wanted anything else. The gentleman next to me commented that the cheese Danish was the best so I ordered one. After one bite I told him that he was right. The counterman smiled and asked if I was new to the area. I told him that it was my first day at my new job at the bank across the street. Are you nervous? Yes, a little. You will be fine. Those are good people to work for. I've been here for over twenty years and know most of them. The only one you have to watch out for is Max Gold. He is the branch manager. Thanks for the advice. The guy next to me slid off his stool and wished me good luck as he left.

I looked at my watch and it was eight twenty five. I paid for my breakfast, left a tip on the counter and walked across the street. I rang the bell and saw someone heading towards the door to let me in. It was the man who had been sitting next to me in the luncheonette a few minutes earlier. Can I help you young man? Yes, I'm Ed Mirabella and I was told to report to Mr. Gold. Come on in. I'm Max Gold and you don't have to watch out for me as long as you do your job. He winked and smiled and asked me to take a seat until the staff came in.

A few minutes later a short stocky woman in her fifties walked over to me and introduced herself. I took particular notice of her eyeglasses that we suspended by a black string that hung around her neck. The glasses rested on a very voluptuous chest and bounced up and down, then left and right as she walked. I was mesmerized and apparently couldn't take my eyes off her chest until she suggested that I look at her face when she spoke. I was jolted back to reality and a little embarrassed as she looked down and placed the eyeglasses back on her nose, the customary place. "Don't worry. I get that all the time.'

CHAPTER FIVE

Annie Baizermann was in charge of the General Cage at the Bensonhurst branch. She had a sweet disposition, but took her training responsibilities very seriously. She would take this young man under her wing and do her very best to prepare him for a permanent assignment that would surely come in the near future.

She would first review all the duties that her little department of three people was responsible for. The word "General" in the title pretty much summed up the role. They booked loans, cut and redeemed coupons for Municipal Bond owners, sold series E Bonds and travelers' checks, purchased and sold foreign currency and processed Night Deposit Bags during an era when the local merchants deposited huge amount of cash over the weekend when all commercial banks were closed. If the Teller lines became too long, one of the cage employees would also accept deposits and cash checks.

In the 1960s, a messenger would pick up the Teller transactions several times a day, and bring them back to Manhattan for processing. Deposit Operations and Check Processing were located in Manhattan and employed hundreds of people who physically handled each check and routed it to the proper bank for payment. If a branch office wasn't in proof by the time the last messenger arrived, someone would have to deliver it after hours. I was handed the bag and carfare many times. The banking industry moved and stored millions of ton of paper every week. It became a labor intense industry that ultimately would use technology to replace the paper, cut costs and unfortunately the people that were necessary to perform those jobs.

As I would soon find out, we could also be called upon to assist the Platform staff when needed. The platform consisted of a long line of desks that lined the wall just inside the main entrance to the bank. The staff consisted of a secretary whose desk was adjacent to the entrance, followed by three or four more desks that were manned, "yes I do mean manned", by junior officers, an Assistant Manager and the Manager. His desk was situated at the extreme back wall and was right next to his personal conference room.

When a customer or prospective customer entered the bank the Secretary would provide a greeting followed by a, "How can we help you today"? She was the so called "gatekeeper" and would try to refer the person to the appropriate desk on the platform for service. The platform assistants were assigned the most menial tasks and the assistant manager would be next in line depending on the situation. The manager should only be bothered for the most important issues that related to the biggest and best customers or a new account that would add significant deposits to the branch. The underlings were well aware of this chain of command. The manager wasn't to be approached by a person that he didn't know. He had more important things to attend to, although I sensed he had little to do most days. If someone managed to get past the secretary and platform staff the private conference room proved to be a convenient place to escape.

I followed Annie around like a playful puppy that first day trying to absorb and retain everything she taught me. I handled each customer transaction with her at my side. She was patient and patted my shoulder each time I completed a task. The morning flew by quickly and now I was told to go to lunch and be back in the branch at one o'clock sharp.

I was more nervous than hungry so I wandered down 86th street for the next hour. The sidewalks were packed with shoppers, mostly women who darted in and out of the local greengrocer, fish store, a bread shop that also sold homemade pasta and so on. Lenny's Pizzeria was next in line and the smell of fresh pizza woke up my appetite. A slice and a coke cost fifteen cents. I ate and walked a little further. Sid's Pants had just opened their first store in Brooklyn, and most of the young men shopped there looking for the latest styles to attract the ladies. On the corner directly across from the bank was Jahn's Ice Cream Parlor, also their first shop in Brooklyn. That chain would grow and prosper for many years. I looked at my father's watch on my left wrist and it was time to go back to work.

The afternoon also went by quickly. My head ached trying to retain all the steps in those paper transactions. At three o'clock I watched the security guard lock the front doors, and stand near them to let the few stragglers leave. I reached for my suit jacket and put it on. Annie looked at me as I walked towards the exit door and waved me back. She whispered, "Where are you going"? I explained my assumption that work was over when the bank closed. She laughed, shook her head and quickly explained that no one goes home until everybody is in proof and the vault is locked. Teller differences had to be found down to the last penny, every cash box had to be locked away along with all the bonds, Travelers checks and loan documents.

I ultimately left the branch at five o'clock only to find a worried Mom waiting for me at home. The following day Bensonhurst lost electric power just before three in the afternoon. As a result we were unable to use our adding machines to prove up. No problem and Annie pulled out the manual cranks that were delivered to the bank along with those machines. We finished the days proof and left the bank just as the power came back. In this modern age we wouldn't be able to do a thing until the power returned. Technology does have its' drawbacks.

Several days after I started working at the branch Mr. Gold summoned me to his desk. He asked me to bring my suit jacket with me. He was alone on the platform and needed me to sit at one of the empty desks until the staff returned from a variety of errands and meetings. He quickly schooled me on what to say and do, and asked the secretary to help me if necessary. Within minutes an elderly woman walked in the door and approached the secretary. The woman spoke in broken English and could not make herself understood. The secretary immediately motioned the woman to my desk. First rule of banking. Don't ass-ume anything or you will probably make and ass out of you and me.

She assumed that because I am Italian, I spoke Italian which was not accurate. I did understand it a little, and the words I knew were the curses and rude expressions that I overheard while growing up. At any rate Mrs. Giordano was introduced to me and sat down on the side chair next to my desk. I was able to decipher that she wanted to apply for a loan to purchase new furniture and needed to borrow eight hundred dollars. The secretary thrust a loan application into my hand and suggested that I fill it out for her. That would not be acceptable in the modern era when someone would most certainly deny any involvement with that application if the loan went bad. In 1963 it was done all the time.

The application looked simple enough calling for basic information like name address, phone number, social security number, date of birth, employment and income. I tried to make the experience pleasant for her and me, and asked what she was going to buy with the money and how long did she need to repay the loan. She answered immediately in broken English that three years would be fine and she held up three fingers to make sure I understood. She went on to explain that she would buy a three piece "sexual" sofa. I immediately said, "You mean, sectional sofa", and she nodded in agreement. I managed to complete the upper part of the application but when I asked for her date of birth I detected a problem.

She was sixty three years of age, and in that era if the loan would mature after an individual exceeded the age of sixty five you could not grant the loan. You assumed that all income other than social security would stop upon reaching retirement and therefore the loan payments would be in jeopardy. That limitation would disappear years later when it was correctly deemed to be discriminatory.

I explained the problem as best I could and saw her facial expression and demeanor undergo a radical change. She put her finger in my face and said the following words in an angry tone. "Mr. Mirabella, my daughter has a "bigga cunda'. You will give me this loan". In one second my inexperience became apparent and panic took over. Was this woman truly referring to a private body part and was I wrong in correcting her when she referred to a "sexual sofa" instead of sectional? Quite possibly. I immediately blurted out what I thought was the Italian expression for "excuse me" and searched out the one person in the bank that might speak the Italian language.

Joe Colucci was the Chief Clerk. He supervised everything that went on behind the scenes. He came to my rescue immediately and spoke fluent Italian. In several minutes he had Mrs. Giordano settled down and smiling again. He asked me to finish the application for her, have her sign it and bring it to him. A minute later she thanked me for my help and left the bank smiling. I was at this point confused and nervous. Joe settled me down as he did with Mrs. Giordano when he explained that her daughter owned a retail shop in the community and she did indeed have a "big account" in the bank. She would be willing to cosign on the loan, making the age of the borrower a moot point. This event has stayed with me for fifty years. It taught me a valuable lesson. Don't lose your cool and don't get involved in situations that you aren't prepared for. In this particular case I didn't have a choice.

Later that day I had the opportunity to listen to a conversation between the branch manager and a customer who distributed olive oil throughout the metropolitan area. The name was one I knew well from newspaper articles that referred to the individual as an "Organized Crime Capo". Bensonhurst was home to a number of reputed mob figures, but some of these people also ran "legitimate" businesses. Mr. Gold was informing the customer about one of his employees who was ninety days past due on his auto loan payments.

It was an acceptable practice back then, and very often produced the desired results. Today it would be looked upon as a violation of the customers' privacy.

The customer politely asked if he could use the phone, dialed his office and asked to speak to the employee. In a calm but stern voice I heard him say; "Joe, this is Mr. P. I'm at the bank and Mr. Gold advised me that there is a problem with your loan. I consider it an embarrassment because I referred you to my bank for financing. Are you trying to ruin my good name"? A rather profound statement from someone who received a lot of attention from the media. He listened for a few seconds and closed out the conversation with, "Not tomorrow. Today before three". Mr. Gold thanked him for his help and the customer apologized for the employees' unacceptable behavior.

Not five minutes later the employee rushed into the bank with a handful of cash. He made the three late payments, and one additional, just in case he forgot again. Mr. Gold looked at him and said. "I don't think you will be forgetting to make your payments on time in the future". He was right of course. Many years later when Mr. Gold retired, a new manager with Italian ancestry was assigned to run the branch. In less than a year that individual was arrested for consorting with known organized crime families. It was simply guilt by association. The man had done nothing wrong and was never charged, indicted or convicted of a crime. His banking career was however over.

His predecessor had managed that facility for many years without incident. This was a stark lesson in reality for me as my career moved forward. It was a time when the Mob attracted more headlines than they wanted, and being Italian was enough to attract a jaundiced eye from the banks. I would on occasion call the security and protection department to do a background check whenever I was involved in a deal that had the slightest chance of being scrutinized, simply based upon Italian ownership. I must state that I was never told to "stay clear" of a deal, but it was wise to take the extra step in the event that something unsavory was unearthed at a later date. Was this an early version of profiling? If it was, it was justified in my opinion.

I had just completed my first week in Bensonhurst and was looking forward to the weekend. On Monday morning I was back at work. The initial jitters were gone and I approached each transaction with some confidence. Annie was always there to answer my questions if I was unsure of myself. I also had the chance to observe all the other employees in the branch and I finally understood just what the Assistant Manager did each day.

CHAPTER SIX

Ruby Kagan stood about five feet four inches, had thinning grey hair combed straight back, and a stocky build. Each morning he would spend the first half hour sitting at his desk reading the New York Times while sipping a cup of coffee. No one should disturb him between eight thirty and nine. Max Gold got away with it because he was the ultimate boss in this branch office that was truly a bank unto itself. You knew when Mr. Gold was kidding if he winked after one of his straight faced jokes. On this particular morning he walked past Kagans' desk and said. "Hey Ruby, why are you reading the Times? Not many pictures in that paper. The New York Post is more your speed". Ruby never looked up.

At nine fifteen the first messenger of the day arrived carrying a huge sack of interoffice mail. Kagan took that sack and dumped it onto his desk and sorted it by department and individual. He was however only looking for one thing and that was the daily overdraft report. The length of that report would dictate whether he would be in a foul mood for the rest of the day. He would look at it one line at a time muttering words like, putz, schmuck, nincompoop, idiot etc. He was of course referring to the various customers that were overdrawn in their checking accounts that morning. He had until two that afternoon to contact each customer that warranted a call and give them the time to come into the branch to make a deposit. If the list was longer than one page his mood became serious. If it exceeded two pages he became totally pissed off. "It's gonna take me all morning to call all these people. Screw it, I'm gonna return this one, and that one. They're overdrawn every day". Max Gold never looked up while Kagan bitched. He kept his face buried deep inside the Wall Street Journal. "What's the matter Ruby? Are they going to interrupt your next coffee break"? Kagan would sit down and pick up his phone to dial those that deserved a call and avoid the embarrassment of having their checks returned.

Occasionally he would listen to the plight of the customer on the other end of the phone line politely. Other times he would respond with the word "bullshit". Next time your checks go back. Many a time he would remind the customer that Hanukah or Christmas was coming, depending on the religion of the person he was speaking with, and they better remember how good he was to them during the year. This particular day was a bad one when the overdraft report exceeded two and a half pages. He might have to eat his lunch at his desk today. Annie reminded me to stay clear of Kagan today, and I did.

The Bensonhurst business district consisted of retail shops that lined both sides of the street. The merchants were predominantly Jewish or Italian as were the employees in the local bank branch. It was common practice to say thank you for a year of good service by presenting your favorite Teller, Clerk of Platform officer with a gift during the holidays. These gestures of good will would ultimately be frowned upon, limited in dollar value and in some cases totally eliminated. A bank Teller could double his annual salary from these gifts that were often in the form of cash. Of course the most generous customers would receive the biggest favors or special treatment when they needed a loan. It was common practice to drop a hint when processing a new loan. "You are a butcher. I bet your steaks are of good quality. This community won't tolerate inferior meat. I should try some of your meat before I make a decision on your loan". Within an hour a bag was delivered to the banker, the loan was funded the next day, and the merchant had been educated.

When Kagan was in a good mood it was a good day for all. He would joke, tease and kid everyone, but paid particular attention to the women. The little guy was happily married, but a bit of a flirt. The girls as he called them would giggle and laugh at his antics when he was in the mood, another "no no" in this day and age, and avoid him like the plague on bad days. He had spent Monday morning lecturing most of the customers that were on the overdraft list, and it produced positive results.

The following morning he walked around the bank holding a single sheet of paper. He was whistling and said a hearty good morning to everyone. Annie looked at him and commented about his good humor. His reply brought a roars of laughter from the women. "Ladies, today I'm blessed with eight inches. That makes me happy every time". He was of course referring to the overdraft list that only covered two thirds of a sheet of paper. He would dispense with that project in an hour or less. "I'll take three coffee breaks today Max". Gold just shook his head and smiled.

That Friday would be my final day in Bensonhurst. I would return there at some point but under different circumstances. For now I was permanently assigned to the Pitkin Avenue branch, deep in the middle of Brownsville, East New York.

I would spend my weekend trying to map out my bus route for Monday morning.

CHAPTER SEVEN

The Pitkin Avenue office was located on the corner of Watkins Street in the middle of a busy retail area. This had been a predominantly Jewish community that was going through some changes. One block away from the branch was Belmont Avenue which was lined with pushcarts during the nineteen twenties. Those pushcarts slowly disappeared when retail shops with apartments above them were constructed in the late twenties and early thirties. Early on the merchants lived above their shops until they were able to buy homes of their own in neighboring residential communities.

A Puerto Rican community was now growing and the old buildings provided affordable rents for these new Americans. The bank branch operated in the same manner as I had experienced in Bensonhurst, but the customer base was almost exclusively Jewish. In nineteen fifty five Bankers Trust had acquired all the assets of the Public National Bank which served the merchant communities in the Bronx, Manhattan and Brooklyn, and boasted the fourth largest branch system in New York. Most of these branch offices were located in thriving Jewish merchant neighborhoods, and as I soon learned, most of the staff could converse in Yiddish and Hebrew. It wasn't unusual to see serial number tattoos on the arms of the men and women who had survived the concentration camps during the Holocaust.

The platform staff comprised of five officer desks and a secretary, identical to the Bensonhurst facility. Joe Brawer was the branch manager who spent most of his day at his desk reviewing credit files and occasionally engaging the most favored customers in conversation. Larry Sandler sat directly in front of him, and it was clear that this young banker was truly favored by the manager.

Next in line was Irving Yofan who spent much of his day working on operational issues and warding off the jokes and ridicule directed at him. He was the oldest of the group and would be looking at retirement in the near future. As a result his career path was all behind him, and his intent was to survive until age sixty five. While most of the jokes were good natured Yofan never disappointed us. He gave us a reason to laugh on a regular basis. One day he came into the office wearing a white sock on one foot and a black one on the other. He stood up most of the day because his pants would cover the obvious mistake. Another day he returned from lunch with brown gravy all over the front of his shirt and tie. Brawer asked him if he enjoyed the brisket sandwich. "It looks good on you Irving." Several weeks later he committed the ultimate blunder arriving at the office with one black shoe with laces and a brown loafer on the other foot. He blamed this error on his wife. "She won't let me turn on the light when I get dressed. It wakes her up." The kidding went on for hours. "Didn't you notice that only one shoe had laces?" "Did you ever think of laying out your clothes the night before?" he walked out of the office that day and didn't return until the following morning.

The fourth desk was occupied by Donald Picker who had spent his earlier days in the bank behind the Teller and General Cage bars. Any advancement in those days was clearly determined by an individuals' ability to perform at a high level and work their way through the entry level positions for many years until someone identified you as candidate for the much coveted platform. Your initial experience gave you the necessary tools to deal with the customer on a face to face basis, and you had, in the eyes of your boss developed the interpersonal skills that were necessary to take on the additional responsibility .Picker had made that transition, and was looked upon as someone who still had room for additional advancement.

The old Public National branches were full of people that started as a messenger before becoming a teller, and some of them spent an entire career in that job. In the nineteen fifties the Depression was still a vivid memory of massive unemployment and bank failures. Doing a good job meant that you would have continuous employment, and that was good enough for most, but not for me. I would work hard, attend college at night and prove to myself and the bosses that I deserved the opportunity to move on and up that ladder of success.

On the other side of the river in Manhattan things operated quite differently. Young men that had graduated from a university would be hired at much higher salaries, trained to lend or handle an investment portfolio for the very rich, and achieve officer titles in one or two years. An Assistant Treasurer in Manhattan was in a different officer category than his peers that worked in the branch system, and through some unfair analysis would be paid approximately ten percent more than his branch counterparts. Many of the officers in the branches were college graduates, but would never see parity with their New York City counterparts, unless of course you were selected to fill a spot in that world, which rarely happened.

Joe Cantwell was just such a person. He had moved up quickly through the branch system and found himself a vice president at a very young age. I remember him visiting the Pitkin Avenue branch one day, and wondered, "Who is this guy anyway"? The men all rose to shake his hand, and the women fawned over him. He was tall, very handsome and dressed in the New York City style; dark suit, white shirt, paisley tie, right down to his wing tip shoes and board room socks. I quickly learned that he had been "one of us" and made that big move into the city. His star would continue to climb as a result of the early experience in the branch system. His associates in headquarters never even visited the other side of the Teller counter and were in my opinion, dry, cold people who tended to look at the rest of us as children of a lesser God. Joe always treated us with respect and provided youngsters like myself with a role model.

At the end of my first week at Pitkin Avenue, I was looking forward to payday. That was the only day of the week when I would not bring lunch from home. The Kosher luncheonette just cross the street from the branch seemed to be a favorite gathering place for the business owners and the bank employees. I would on this Friday treat myself to a deli sandwich and a bottle of Dr. Browns' cream soda. I was looking for an empty seat at the counter when the Head Teller at the branch invited me to share a small table with him. In that era he was a big man in the branch, responsible for hundreds of thousands of dollars and eight tellers. I was flattered and joined him.

The lunch special in those days was less expensive because it was from the previous day's menu. It happened to be brisket of beef which I considered a Jewish form of pot roast, and a favorite of mine. I already knew that day old lasagna tasted much better than the day it was cooked because it had time to marinate and merge all the component flavors. In our current environment a restaurant will present the specials verbally and the pricing for these items is usually higher. At any rate I devoured my sandwich along with the half sour pickle that was recommended and washed it down with my cream soda. That lunch cost me $1.25 with a tip. I could still get two slices of pizza and a coke for fifty cents in 1963, but I felt I deserved a better lunch that day. Of course, lunch with another person results in lots of conversation. Before the end of that day I would learn a few other things that would make my lunch a distant memory.

CHAPTER EIGHT

I returned to the cage after lunch that Friday with a full belly and the feeling that I had made a new friend. The head teller asked me lots of questions about the hiring process and of course my starting salary. I answered that last question, but shouldn't have. It revealed that I was making ten dollars a week more than he was, and it didn't take him five minutes to complain about it after we returned to the office. At the end of the day I was called out to the platform by the branch manager and he didn't look happy. I was the new kid and this was not the way to impress the superiors. "You never discuss your salary with other employees, young man. Now I have a bigger problem because he is threatening to quit if I don't give him a raise immediately". No explanation for my actions would be heard and I returned to my cage wondering if I would be fired because of this serious infraction. I wasn't fired and worked at that branch for another year when I was offered a transfer.

Fitting in is enough of a problem for a new employee but it is even more difficult when there are cultural differences to deal with at the workplace. I was one of two non-Jews working there. Many of the customers were reluctant to deal with the "goyem or gentile" as I was called. I worked hard without another incident, but never felt accepted. I received a minimal raise at the end of that year and the next one.

The 1965 Christmas holiday passed and like most twenty two year olds I was looking forward to New Years' Eve with my family and friends. Plans were made to meet at a local restaurant for dinner around nine. It was a work day and I casually asked if we would be allowed to leave a bit early. I was not so casually reminded that each branch had to close out the books for the year end before I could leave. I was way down the seniority list and watched as the senior workers left at four that afternoon. Murphy's Law took over and everything was out of proof. I muddled through the various differences and I was out the door around seven thirty, with enough time to get home, change clothes and get to the restaurant shorty after nine.

A week later I would be notified to report to the branch located on Graham Avenue and Varet Street, also in East New York. It was now 1966, I was married and would become a father for the first time in February.

Irving Friedman greeted me at the entrance to the Graham Avenue office and directed me to have a seat at his desk. He was the manager of the facility which housed some of the largest account relationships in all of Brooklyn. This was a totally different environment from my prior assignment and I had a good feeling about it from day one. I tried to explain my decision to transfer but was stopped by a hand and an outstretched arm. "Eddie, this is your first day in my branch and nothing from the past matters to me. I will only evaluate how you work for me. Good luck and go see Bob. He runs the cage". I went to work and never looked back because I began to see a future in banking.

Six months later Bob resigned to accept a position at another bank. I was put in charge of the cage with a promise of a raise to compensate me for the additional work and responsibility. When the raise finally came I was disappointed but kept my mouth shut. I did discuss the matter with Saul Greenberg the assistant manager who advised me to wait for the right opportunity to bring it up. What's the right opportunity Mr. Greenberg? "You will know Eddie, you will know". Several months later a situation developed which became the perfect opportunity for me to discuss the raise issue.

As I mentioned earlier, the Graham Avenue branch was the home of some of the largest and most profitable account relationships outside of Manhattan. The senior lenders for the bank were often seen meeting with Friedman and these premier clients. When Harry Tappan or Irving Volen were coming for a visit the entire staff would be told, "Dress nice for Mr. Volen ladies. Eddie, get a haircut before Friday. You too Saul, and everybody keep the suit jackets on all day." Irv Volen became a legend in the industry having financed the growth of so many businesses. I remember being told many stories about his ability to put his arms around a business or a concept and see the opportunity for the customer and the bank. Yes, I did say "concept".

One such concept involved a new business that had designed an artificial sweetener that had a wide range of possible uses. Saccharin tablets had been around forever and would be used in coffee or tea, and from my perspective, tasted horrible. This new product could be sprinkled on cereal or fruit and used in baking and cooking. In normal situations the bank would not be interested in this new venture, but the prospective client was introduced by a major client in the food industry who had known the individual and his family for years. Ultimately the loan was approved and "Sweet and Low" was born. Character and Capacity had been identified and quantified. This is only one of thousands of such examples.

In those days it was more important early on in the process to know more about you, the businessman, than what you do. If a new client was introduced to the bank by a respected customer the initial road blocks were few. It someone walked in without an introduction, it became a priority to reach out to other customers or suppliers in the same industry for their opinion as it related to their character and capacity. Very early in this writing I mentioned the five C's of credit. The remaining three would not matter if a customer failed to pass the character and capacity tests. In this modern age financial analysis is the catalyst for all loans. If the numbers make sense a deal happens. I have seen many instances where the credit was strong but the loan went bad, because of the absence of good character, and the lack of deep pockets which ultimately defines capacity.

My mother always used the phrase, "Show me your company and I'll tell you what you are". She used it in conjunction with my choice of friends during my youth, and it made a lot of sense. If I hung out with hoods, I would be cast into their lot. The same analysis holds true in business. The old time bankers knew how to size up an individual before making any judgment based on the financial statements or tax returns. It worked for them back then, but would never be allowed in the present. How sad.

State and Federal regulations have tied the hands of bankers to a point where it is difficult to do business in the normal sense. The new normal tells the people that provide financing to walk away from any transactions that are the least bit out of the ordinary. Character loans are a thing of the past. One of my favorite "character" comments came from Irv Friedman when he described a customer as, "the type of guy who will pay his bills before he buys groceries for his family".

CHAPTER NINE

Early one morning the president of a candy manufacturing company stopped by the branch to ask for a short term loan. He needed two hundred thousand dollars to finance a large order he had received from a retailer. He would need to boost his inventory of raw materials to complete the order and would be paid within thirty days after delivery. Mr. Friedman pulled out the credit file to check on the status of the existing line of credit, prepared a promissory note for the client to sign and told the customer that the money would be in his account that day. He then dictated a memo for the file to his secretary and delivered the note to me for processing. The last thing he did was erase the notation in the upper right hand corner of the document and change the interest rate from 4 3/4% to 5%.

I booked the loan and mailed out a confirmation to the customer for his file. Several days later the client came in waving the confirmation in front of Friedmans' face while complaining about the interest rate. "I always pay prime rate. This note shows a rate of prime plus ¼%". He was visibly angry and felt that the bank didn't appreciate his business and very large checking account. Friedman saw me standing at my window and motioned me out to the platform. He turned the focus of the conversation in my direction and berated me in front of the customer, the platform staff and anyone else that was in hearing range. He finished his tirade with a statement that placed all the blame on me, causing him tremendous embarrassment with a major account. "Correct this transaction immediately", and with a wave of his arm I was dismissed and returned to the cage.

I was shaken from the embarrassing attack that I had just experienced but went to work and made the adjustment to the interest rate. Another client might have dismissed the small upward adjustment in the rate without a thought. This client didn't achieve his great success without watching every expense category and the last minute change did not go unnoticed. At the end of the day I left the office without saying the traditional goodnight and called in ill the next morning. I went into Manhattan and filed an application at Chase Manhattan. I was interviewed that same morning and offered a position at fifteen dollars a week more. I accepted the offer and went home to write my resignation letter. I would report for work at Chase after tending the customary two weeks' notice.

The following morning was a Friday and I arrived at the office a little earlier than usual. Saul Greenberg was always the first to arrive as it was his responsibility to unlock the doors and conduct an inspection of the premises. He was opening the main door as I arrived and let me in. "Hey Eddie, you're not going to do anything rash because of what happened, are you"? No Saul, I'm just going to resign. I placed the envelope that contained my resignation on Friedmans' desk and went directly to my work station. "I think you're making a mistake". No, Friedman made the mistake and then compounded it by blaming it on me. I won't accept treatment like that from anyone.

When Friedman arrived Saul got up from his desk and disappeared down the stairway that led to the coffee room and the bathrooms. He didn't want to be sitting there when that envelope was opened. He was right. Friedman called me out to his desk, held up the resignation letter and tore it into pieces. "I'm not accepting your resignation. Now go do your work and I'll talk to you at three when the bank closes". I looked at him in disbelief and as I turned to walk away, found myself telling him that ripping up the letter didn't change anything and I was leaving in two weeks. No response this time, but I did detect a look of discomfort on his face.

At 3:05 that afternoon I followed him down to the coffee room in the basement. He sat down at the table across from me and his tone had completely changed. I was told that I was a valuable member of the staff, always went above and beyond in my job, and that he didn't want me to leave. He also tried to convince me that he couldn't admit to the interest rate adjustment because he as the branch Manager would look bad. It was easier to blame it on someone else. As ridiculous as it sounds it made sense to me at the time.

I wasn't letting him off the hook that easily and used the moment to tell him about my dissatisfaction with my last raise. I have a wife and child at home and at this rate I'll be fifty before I'm earning a decent salary. I work hard because I want advancement opportunities as well as a decent salary. He just looked at me for a few seconds and finally agreed to address all my issues. "Now will you rescind your resignation"? Let me think about it over the weekend and let's see what issues you can deal with by Monday. When I left the coffee room he was still sitting at the table. As I climbed the stairs I heard him say, "I apologize, and don't resign".

The weekend went by so slowly for me. I wanted to settle the issue, but I also knew that I didn't want to resign. I liked my job and the people I was working with. I had also been raised to admit to my mistakes but fight like hell when I was right. I did the latter and it looked like I may have won the battle. I also knew that Friedman was thinking about the same things and he may decide that he doesn't want a fighter on his staff. In those days employees had too few rights and nowhere to go if they were mistreated or wrongfully judged.

Monday arrived soon enough and I found Curt Campbell waiting to see me when I arrived at the office. Curt was the operations deputy that reported directly to Jim Clifford who had hired me three years earlier. I assumed that he was there to accept my resignation and tell me to go home now. As I've said many times, "never assume". We met in the conference room and I listened in disbelief. I would be promoted to Platform Assistant within a month. My salary would be adjusted for merit and promotion. Within six months you will be assigned to a new branch that the bank is building in Bay Ridge as second in charge and will be promoted again to Assistant Manager if you continue to perform at a high level. "The bank now has a tuition reimbursement plan Ed. Are you still taking classes"? Yes I am sir, and that would be the only time I spoke until I said "thank you".

As I stepped out of the conference room Irv Friedman was standing there with Saul Greenberg at his side. They were both smiling. I was holding back tears. As I said on Friday Eddie, I'm not accepting your resignation. I'm not resigning anymore Mr. Friedman. I returned to my station and worked at a feverish pace that day. My adrenalin was pumping and I couldn't wait to go home and share my news with my family. Lord knows, I wasn't much fun to be with over the previous weekend. Within two weeks my replacement reported to the branch and I would now occupy a desk on the platform. I had achieved my initial goal in three years and felt confident about my future.

I can still remember the first time I sat in that big chair. I had my own phone to my left, two file boxes marked "In and Out" on the right and a green blotter wrapped with leather borders sat in the middle. The chair swiveled and tilted back. This was great I thought until I leaned too far back and tipped over. I was embarrassed and the rest of the staff thought it was hilarious. In the middle of my desk I found two small cardboard boxes. One contained business cards that bore the name of the bank, the address, phone number and right in the middle was my name and title. The other box was heavy to the touch. I acted like a kid opening presents on Christmas morning. "Gee, what could it be"? I opened the box and held up a solid bronze name plate that had to weigh three pounds. It had green felt on the bottom to protect the wooden surface of the desk, and across the front it said, MR. MIRABELLA. I placed it on the right hand corner of the desk and found myself staring at it when I heard a voice yell out. "Turn it around you putz, the customers are supposed to see it". I laughed at myself this time.

Mr. Greenberg took me to lunch that day to celebrate my new position and with that lunch came words of advice. "You are sitting at that front desk. It's your job to identify and qualify each new face that comes in the door. The big accounts will walk right past you and come to me or Friedman. The people that look lost or uncertain are the ones that you handle. Of course if someone wants to open a new account and it looks like something substantial I want you to introduce me after the paperwork is completed of course. I will then determine if they should meet Friedman. Got it"? I nodded in agreement and continued to listen. He talked about the new special checking account service that the bank would launch. "You mean everybody can have a checking account"? Yes, and we collect a monthly fee and another ten cents for each check they write. We also charge them for printed checkbooks.

All the employees would also get a "free" checking account and our pay would be deposited into it on payday. "What will they think of next"? Don't tell anybody but they are looking to keep the branches open late one or two nights a week for the commuter who can't make it to the bank by three. If it becomes official I hear they will pay you overtime and give you three dollars for supper money. You could eat for a buck and a half and pocket the rest. Not bad huh"? In those days you couldn't walk into another branch of the bank and expect to get service. All your records and signature cards were kept in one place only, and that was at your branch. If one of our customers stopped by a branch in Manhattan to cash a check, it was necessary to call my branch to discuss the transaction, have the account officer speak with the client on the phone and ultimately approve or deny the transaction. Banking was starting to evolve.

CHAPTER TEN

During the next few months Irv Friedman took me with him on calls at least twice a week. "Eddie, sit and listen. Don't say shit. You understand"? Just listen and ask me questions when we get back in the car. I followed his lead and kept my mouth shut on the first call. It was an all day road trip to visit a knit goods manufacturer that had relocated to Penn Argyle Pennsylvania. During the long car ride I listened intently as Irv explained the history of this very profitable company. The double knit business was in its infancy and this customer had no real competition. The bank was now concerned about our ability to visit with the customer on a quarterly basis. This was a substantial borrower during the sixties, when the outstanding loan balance would exceed one million dollars. Irv Volen made Friedman promise to visit them quarterly and document the call in a memo for the credit file. Friedman always kept his promises.

On the way back to the branch I was asked to take out a pad and pen. Friedman would dictate the memo to me to pass the time. When we returned to the branch I would type it with two carbon copies. The original went to the credit file, one copy was sent to Volen and the third copy was for me. Why me, sir? "Cause you're gonna sign it Eddie". I remembered all too well the promissory note incident. He looked at me for a second and explained that he wanted to show that he was providing me with the basic ability to deal with major customers. It will help you in the future. "I won't always be here, you

58

know"! I nodded and waited for him to start dictating.

Anyone with an ounce of sense would realize that I may have typed the memo, but the wording was not mine. Friedman was the Jewish Street banker. I was the young Italian kid. We spoke differently and the first line of the memo clearly reflected that difference. "Today me and Irv Friedman went to visit our customer in Pennsylvania. Rained so hard we shoulda took a boat". I shook my head. He noticed and asked me, "You gotta problem with that"? No sir, and he continued. He went on to outline the tour of the new plant, the new circular knitting machines that helped cut payroll expenses by forty percent, and the finished product, "a nice sweater". From wool to a garment in five minutes.

Now it was time to end the memo, and somewhere during his many years in banking he picked up one line that would emphasize his strong feelings for this customer. "Predicated on the aforementioned, we have no hesitancy in going along". What's that mean Mr. Friedman? It means we're gonna lend them more money. Several days later I received a call from Irv Volen. "Nice memo Eddie. When did you become Jewish? Are you circumcised too"? No Mr. Volen, I'm Italian. We prefer to wear it off. He laughed and asked to speak to Friedman. I transferred the call.

The following week we visited with the candy manufacturer that was so pissed at me several weeks back. Alex greeted Friedman like he was God. I started to understand the level of respect between customer and "their" banker. It's a partnership of sorts. You lend me the money to make more money and I pay you back with interest. The relationship grew over decades where trust was established through consistent performance. I'm starting to really grasp the C in

Now Alex saw me standing in the doorway looking very uncomfortable. "Eddie, come in, sit down. I'm not gonna bite you. No hard feelings. In fact I respect that you try to make a few extra bucks for the bank. Just don't do it with my money". They laughed and I sat down. Years later, Alex would be my customer when I became manager of the Maspeth Queens branch. I would receive the same respect that Mr. Friedman got. I was also the recipient of gifts during the holidays when he said Happy Holidays to every employee in the branch, with a small token gift. By that time the bank had issued a policy putting a limit on what could be accepted.

In the spring of 1967 Irv Friedman took me to lunch to say "so long". I was being transferred to the new branch that was under construction in Bay Ridge Brooklyn. "You will do well Eddie and I'm not in the least, worried about you". Starting on Monday you report to Max Gold in Bensonhurst. Do you know him? Yes I do. I spent several weeks there when I first joined the bank. That branch is only a few miles from the new location. That will be your base of operation. You should be promoted to Assistant Manager within six months. If not, Friedman's coming to kick your ass".

Back in Bensonhurst the following Monday, I was greeted like a homecoming hero. Annie was so proud of the little "pisha" she had trained. Max and Ruby wanted to hear about the new branch, but mostly about my years with Irv Friedman. In their eyes my career was moving forward at lightning speed. I would open the new branch a few months later, and be promoted within six months.

The bank was opening new locations every few months during the late 1960s and continued to do so into the mid-seventies.

CHAPTER ELEVEN

The Bay Ridge office opened in the fall of 1967 with much fanfare and hoopla. We had spent the entire summer visiting prospective customers throughout the business community. We focused on the attorneys because they could generate huge account balances in those days, along with the insurance agencies. Retail stores were next in line, although they deposited large amounts of cash on a daily basis. They also filled the branch with employees each Friday to cash their paychecks. Almost immediately the new branch offered nighttime hours on Monday and Friday. I loved the overtime it generated, especially during the first month of operation when we were open from nine in the morning through nine at night.

That first month also coincided with the bank holding a campaign to generate new business. The employees were rewarded for each new account opened with points that could be redeemed for everything from appliances to house wares and jewelry. I had recently purchased my first home and was able to furnish most of it with the prizes I selected including my first console color television. Several months later I was promoted to assistant branch manager and found the promotion to be bitter sweet. I became an exempt employee which was defined as a salaried position regardless of the hours worked.

Simply put, no more overtime. The raise I received with the promotion was far less than I had received in overtime payments.

Several months later the bank issued its' first credit card. They named it the BankAmericard which evolved into today's Visa. Commercial banking was turning into a supermarket of financial services. Unfortunately many of the new services were riddled with service issues, sparking a comment from Gordon Woodward an Executive Vice President. "We should stop bringing new services on line until we figure out how to service the ones we have now". I'm sure that comment wasn't warmly received back at 16 Wall Street.

In 1969 the Vietnam War was winding down and the bank was hiring returning veterans in large numbers. Many of them were college graduates, and they were put on a fast track training program. I was asked to provide that training for the veterans that would be assigned to work in the Brooklyn branches. One problem erupted almost immediately. These new employees were also fast tracked for promotions, and people like myself were passed over for branch manager assignments. I voiced my complaint, saw nothing was done about it, and resigned a year later.

Timing is everything in life, and this decision was made at the worst possible time. Soon after joining a smaller bank I separated from my wife and started wading through the divorce process. The stress of a new job combined with a marital breakup was reflected in my performance. A little more than a year later I found myself back at 16 Wall Street asking for my old job. I was quickly rehired and assigned to a branch in the Flatlands Section of Brooklyn, as an assistant manager. I would have to serve my penance for leaving before I would be looked upon as a candidate for any upward moves.

Most of the returning veterans that I trained had already accepted positions with other banks or in some cases went to work for the government. Their initial employment at Bankers Trust was nothing more than a stepping stone. Business experience combined with a college education made them attractive candidates to recruiters.

The bank was now experimenting with a new concept referred to as "mini branches". I was selected to manage one located in Brighton Beach. These smaller locations were located in leased premises where the bank could re-evaluate their value after five years. The old Ebinger Bakery chain was shutting down and the retail store space could easily be converted. If a mini branch proved to be profitable it would be easy to expand it into a full service location. Dozens were opened and only one warranted expansion at the end of the first five year lease. Branch banking was becoming over saturated and the times were about to change again.

At the end of 1975 I was transferred to a full size branch in Maspeth Queens as branch manager and within a year was promoted to Assistant Treasurer. I had finally infiltrated the officer ranks at Bankers Trust. I was living in Farmingdale at the time, and the daily commute was tough, but then again gasoline was a lot less expensive.

The Maspeth assignment enabled me to prove myself as an administrator. I inherited a good staff and was able from the onset to leave the branch each day for the purpose of calling on existing customers and prospects. By 1976 the branch manager had little authority left. All lending decisions were made at regional lending offices, and overdrafts were handled in much the same way. We could still cash checks for existing customers, but now we had goals to cross sell new services, and bring in new business. New deposits were still driven by loans, and the regional lending officers were readily available to assist when an opportunity came our way. I kept a manila folder that contained blank, but signed promissory notes in my desk for each borrowing account. It was something that many branch managers did in those days to avoid unnecessary trips to get the note signed when a borrowing need arose. In a few years that practice would be eliminated when a less than honest account officer used the signed notes to book loans and help himself to the proceeds.

The culprit was caught and prosecuted, and most of the money was recovered. New procedures outlined the penalty for anyone caught holding blank signed notes in the future. Termination was the initial price paid for the infraction. The bank might also pursue further legal action if it suffered a financial loss. The industry policed itself and made the appropriate adjustments to policy. Today we have regulators doing all of that for us. As a result of increased regulatory intervention, authority to do anything at the branch level would be taken away in a few short years. Branch personnel would be assigned sales goals when they weren't servicing the customers. Each person sitting on the Platform was now trained to recognize opportunities to cross sell additional services to existing customers.

I didn't wait for opportunities. I created them. I joined the local Kiwanis Club and attended their monthly meetings. I was immediately befriended by the local savings bank managers. In the mid-seventies commercial banks didn't provide residential mortgage services and the savings banks couldn't provide commercial loan services. The referral steam was mutually beneficial to both sides. I also got involved in the local chamber of commerce and quickly realized that I found the same familiar faces at all of these meetings.

The commercial lenders that were assigned to my branch were only too willing to work with me and taught me how to spread financial statements and assist me in writing the various memos that would ultimately be the basis for a credit file. I was becoming a well-rounded banker and the communication skills that I developed as a small boy assisting my deaf mother enabled me to establish "credibility" with my customer base and prospective clients.

I also believed that a "good offense was the best defense". The competition was busy defending itself, and had little time to go after my client base. Their customers didn't know that they were unhappy until I showed them the difference. Those were times when a business owner stayed with a particular bank for decades. They were loyal and the bank knew that. Complacency set in and I was always ready to expose that weakness. My branch excelled in new business, cross sell to existing customers, and my operations staff kept the auditors happy. Just when the engine was humming on all eight cylinders, the industry would begin a new renaissance.

CHAPTER TWELVE

Fifteen years of expansion started to unwind in the late seventies. Bank were located like gas stations on every corner. The market was getting smaller and the economy was weak. It was 1977 and Bankers Trust announced that were exiting retail banking. They had found a suitor who wanted to acquire the branch network. A meeting was called at 270 Park Avenue and the officers were introduced to representatives from Bank of Montreal. We were advised that nothing would change other than the name above the door. Well, nothing did change because the deal unraveled as quickly as it came together.

Whenever the news gets out that a bank is looking to divest, the first thing that happens is "nothing". The lenders immediately try to shore up the weaker credits, new loan approvals fall off dramatically and the branch staff concentrates on keeping its' customer base, and the auditors happy. In my case an accountant that I had worked with became aware of a new frontier for commercial banks on Long Island. Expansion in that market was just beginning and a person with my experience and talents was in demand. I accepted an interview with a senior vice president at the Long Island National Bank of Hicksville and joined their staff in 1978.

I did what anyone else would do and announced my new position as assistant vice president in charge of Business Development to all of my contacts immediately. I was respected not only for the service I had provided as a branch manager, but also as an individual that had no problem fighting for a deal and a customer that I believed in. Almost immediately I began to move some customer accounts and loans to this little community bank that provided "seed loans" to farmers during its early years. First National had been acquired by the Long Island Trust Company in Garden City, but continued to operate separately during the next two years before it was merged into the Garden City organization.

Loan committee met once each month and I would be invited to present the credit requests that emanated from the new clients that I brought to the bank. I was batting one thousand at the end of the first three months and my ability and results were noticed by the chairman of Long Island Trust company. He would attend each loan committee meeting and a few months later I was transferred to Garden City to form a new department that would focus on business development. It was to my knowledge non-existent in the Long Island market to have a dedicated staff promoting new business opportunities for the bank. I will take credit for the concept and its success.

The lending officers would be free to pay closer attention to the existing customer base, their credit needs and to cross sell ancillary services. My group would develop new prospects, evaluate their banking needs and pre-qualify any loan requests before the lenders were brought in. Senior management was committed to the concept and gave me all the tools I needed to do the job. Each year we generated significant new business earnings to the bottom line, and gave the competition "fits". The large banks were still in the throes of reorganizing, divesting and or merging. We had little trouble in attracting and garnering those clients that we targeted. Our lenders could put deals together quickly, get them approved and issue a commitment letter in a week or less. When the big banks started to downsize and divest themselves of the cumbersome branch system, I suggested that the bank entertain the idea of opening a new branch facility in Queens. This was initially considered heresy because we're a Long Island bank and had no knowledge of the Queens market. I was asked to make a presentation to senior management and ultimately received the approval to move forward. The big banks were applying their efforts in the relatively new Long Island market in an effort to escape the overbanked regions of Brooklyn and Queens. Their customers were unhappy and we were going to provide an alternative.

My research centered on the Long Island City, Maspeth border which encompassed several square miles of industry. I also recommended that we staff the location with a regional lending facility that would enable us to act and react quickly to client loan requests. In those days the banks accepted a three year period to achieve breakeven before a new facility became profitable. We were profitable at the end of the first year, which was unheard of at the time. We could open accounts and process loan requests quickly before the competition could react. Our lenders still had the authority to approve loans, and we could join together and combine our credit authorities to approve larger loans. The new concept worked so well that the bank opened another combined branch / lending facility on Long Island a year later.

Things were going so well until;

CHAPTER THIRTEEN

Long Island Trust Company was attracting a lot of attention during this growth period. It was acquired by an Italian bank during the early 1980s, but continued to operate independently for the next few years. The industry was just starting to focus on technology as a means to reduce costs, reduce personnel levels and increase the bottom line substantially. Check processing departments that employed thousands were being re-tooled with equipment that could scan thousands of items in minutes. Credit scoring was replacing the lenders that permeated the retail services spectrum. Everything from installment loans through residential mortgages could be processed and finalized with far fewer people.

Long Island Trust was no different, and spent many millions of dollars developing a new computer system that would meet the needs of an expanding financial services market, while reducing the overhead substantially. Unfortunately a commitment of this size effectively cut into the bottom line, causing concern to the Italian owners. In the space of three years the bank was sold to Bank of New York at a substantial profit.

Almost immediately after the news hit, offers from competing banks started to erupt. The Long Island Trust staff was targeted based upon their reputation. One savings bank hired an entire group of lenders in an effort to provide commercial services to their existing customer base. It didn't work because the savings bank hierarchy did not understand commercial lending. Two years later all of those people that mutinied were looking for jobs. They had attracted a lot of attention when they resigned en mass several years earlier and the memory of "the Garden City Mutiny" was fresh in the minds of an industry that still demanded "some loyalty".

I had learned the hard way to choose my own path in business. Be a leader, not a follower, and call my own shots. I reached out to one person only, at one bank, when I concluded that the sale of Long Island Trust was not beneficial to Ed Mirabella. His name is Frank, and I called him on a Friday. Frank was quickly becoming a legend at the old Chemical Bank. His division encompassed Brooklyn, Queens, Nassau and Suffolk Counties. I had a fair amount of success in attracting significant new business for Long Island Trust by prospecting Chemical Bank customers. In the late nineteen eighties, the levels of bureaucracy made it difficult for lenders to get deals approved. All real estate transactions had to be approved by a separate division. Make no mistake, the deals got done, but the amount of time it took to review and approve a request was frustrating to the customer and the loan officer. "I can't get an answer from my bank", was the one comment I heard over and over.

At Long Island Trust I was able to "walk a deal" around the bank and discuss the loan before spending valuable time on financial statement analysis. My philosophy was simple. A client deserves and appreciates a quick "no", versus "no answer". In a few days I would be able to advise my client of the banks interest, outline the steps to be taken for approval, or advise them to look for another banking source. The prospect that got a "no" from me, appreciated the quick turnaround, and the explanation for the banks negative decision. My reputation in the business community was just as important to me as was the banks' image.

Frank admired my tenacity and made me an offer immediately. I tendered my resignation and reported to Chemical Bank in February of 1987. What I experienced during the first few months was pure and simple "culture shock". I had accepted a position with a bank that had been my primary target during my days with LITCO. I was confident in my own capabilities, but I didn't have confidence in getting my deals approved. As a business development professional, I was often looked upon as a "salesman". A person who was paid to open doors for the lenders, who were now called Relationship Managers. These people had a jaundiced view of lending, and on more than one occasion I was told that Chemical Bank had the distinction of saying "no" to every business on Long Island, at least once.

I immediately started to question my decision to join this large financial institution, and wondered if I had made the same mistake all over again, remembering my hasty resignation from Bankers Trust back in the late nineteen sixties. This time there was no going back. Long Island Trust didn't exist and Bank of New York had its' own way of doing things that emanated from its' founder Alexander Hamilton. The story as I remember it unfolded when Hamilton was leaving the bank one day to participate in the infamous gun duel that ultimately took his life. It was rumored that he told the bank employees to do "nothing" until he returned later that day. Well, he never did return from that duel, and the bank remained unchanged for the next two hundred years.

I was also 44 years of age and needed to start thinking about a vested pension and retirement with benefits for life, which Chemical still offered in the late nineteen eighties. I muddled through the bureaucracy and found a way to not only survive, but was able to achieve some degree of success by bringing several large account relationships into the bank during my first year. That's when I received a short handwritten note from Frank that said "keep up the good work". He recognized my accomplishments in a tough environment, and that's all a person needs to move forward. I was no longer "just a salesman". I was now defined as a salesman that could "deliver".

In 1989 the Long Island market along with much of the country went through some tough times. The real estate market crumbled as did a number of banks. It became almost impossible to get anything done. The Federal government was pointing their arthritic fingers in every direction, and had no problem accusing the banks of wrongdoing. A large number of savings banks failed, and many of them were merged into the large money center banks, who would work out the bad loans that had permeated the industry. The late eighties was my earliest recollection of a time when the banks were targeted for bad lending practices which resulted in far too many bad loans. We lived with constant news reports about the Resolution Trust Company, an arm of the Federal government and their efforts to dissolve hundreds of banks that were deemed insolvent, by a group of reactionaries, who couldn't manage the federal budget, but thought that they were qualified to decide which bank would live and which would die. The government was masterful in deflecting public attention and scrutiny away from themselves by targeting those "fat, rich" bankers. "Ah, the best defense is a good offense". As I said in my prologue; it's a shame that we can't hold our government officials to the same standards that they demand from the banks. Not yet, anyway.

The early nineties was a time to sell everything but loans if you worked for a bank. Cash management services, payroll services, estate and trust services, and the list goes on. We would be fee driven, and if we did make a loan it would only happen after nauseating analysis, careful review, careful review again, to make sure that we didn't miss the one detail that would enable the bank to say "NO". The industry was under so much fire that we looked to pour cold water on the best lending opportunities. Bankers are risk takers, and we price a loan based on risk, term and purpose. Our capitalistic society grew and prospered because of risk takers. Government doesn't understand that concept and it never will.

They just "tax and spend", and if it doesn't achieve the initial goal, well they tax and spend again. They cover their incompetence by targeting a business or industry at regular intervals to deflect attention from their own failures. I'm talking about the late eighties and the early nineties, but it might as well be today. The banks have always been an easy target, because our government likes to cast our proud profession into the category identified as the "rich". The left side of the aisle has no problem attacking the rich as often as possible. It wins elections because most of the people in this country are employed by people that they would define as being "rich". They built businesses, hired people, paid salaries, endured taxes and constant government regulations and intervention, but are hated by most of the population just because they are "rich".

Maybe it's time to remind the population that most if not all of those politicians would fall into that same category. Oh I forgot that they accumulated their wealth honestly. President Bush was attacked by the left for being wealthy, Oops, I meant Rich. The Kennedys however, a proud family that generated its' wealth through the import of liquor is never attacked. I guess that booze is acceptable and oil isn't. Our current president is indeed a wealthy man, but he isn't categorized as rich because he earned his money the right way.

At any rate the banking industry survived the meltdown of the late eighties and before I realized it that same government that attacked the industry was demanding that we lend again and while you're at it, loosen up a little. Here we go again.

CHAPTER FOURTEEN

During the mid-nineties Chemical Bank completed the first of two mega mergers. The first with Manufacturers Hanover was touted as a merger of equals, and we were advised to tell the customer base that it would be "seamless". It actually turned out that way, and the two banks complemented each other in most areas of service. I worked well with the lending officers from both banks and concentrated my business development efforts in Nassau County. Now in my early fifties I was asked to attend the banks advanced credit training program, and attended the three day "boot camp" in New Jersey. I enjoyed the experience despite that fact that I was at least twenty years older than the other participants. I was teamed up with a young lady from Chemical Japan who spoke about three words of English. Somehow we made a respectable presentation for the mythical client that we represented and kept in touch for the next several years.

Soon after Chemical merged with Chase, and for this banker it was not an enjoyable experience. The culture was very different with representatives of both banks jockeying for key positions. I now reported to two different masters which was difficult. I still reported to my old Chemical boss, but I was now expected to serve the needs of the Chase region headed by an individual who truly believed that he was an expert in every facet of banking including business development. The man was a legend in his own mind. I had always been left alone to do my job, and performed well that way. After six months of dealing with his pure lunacy I had a decision to make. I would have to strangle the son of a bitch or resign. I chose the latter and raised my hand for early retirement. I made an appointment to speak with the division head and told him that "Frank" had made a comment regarding early retirement several months earlier, and I wanted to accept the offer. I was flattered by his effort to talk me out of it, but I told him that my decision was final.

Several months later I ran into Frank and told him that I had decided to accept his offer and had spoken to the division head about it. He knew nothing about that conversation, but would look into it. Several days later I received a hand written note from Frank wishing me good luck. He also referred to me as "one of my best hires". I would have to say that he was the best "manager" that I ever worked for. He left you alone to do the job, always found the time to chat with you on work related matters, and supported his staff. During my nine years at Chemical / Chase I never heard a word of criticism directed at him. Many in this industry would do well to take a page from his book.

I had made many friends during my thirty three years in banking and thought about doing some consulting until I was old enough to collect social security and several small pensions. I needed to work, that's for sure. I had put some money aside to tide me over until my consulting business grew, but within weeks of my decision to leave my phone started to ring. The word had gotten out that Ed Mirabella was retiring from Chase, and I received several offers from other banks. Some of those offers came from youngsters that I had trained over the years, and they had all achieved a respectable level of success. I had a simple philosophy with all of them. "Watch how you treat people on your way up, because you never know who you will meet on your way down".

One of those youngsters was the senior trust officer at The First National Bank of Long Island. He reached out to me and suggested that I call the CEO and make an appointment to meet with him. I had worked for him back in the late seventies at the Long Island National Bank of Hicksville. He had in fact hired me.

Bill never made a quick decision in his life and we talked for what seemed like an eternity over the next few months before he made an offer. He wanted me of course, to chat with two senior officers that I would report to and those meetings went well. I had been given a start date, cleared various security checks, and only needed to meet with my direct supervisor, a guy I'll call Moe. What a prick, he turned out to be! It was 1997.

We met for breakfast at a diner on Glen Cove Road in Carle Place on a Monday morning. As soon as I sat down at the table the waitress was there to take my order. Moe didn't look happy from the outset, and made his feelings very clear during the next ten minutes when our breakfast came to an abrupt end. "I have no idea why we are meeting. You were hired without my approval, and I wasn't even consulted or included in the discussion. This is a bad way to start a new job, but that's the way I feel". I just stared at him as he went on, and on. To say the least, I didn't get that "warm fuzzy feeling" from our initial meeting.

Moe finished his coffee, paid the check and said, "See you next Monday", as he got up and left me sitting there. I had become a pawn in some kind of political battle and I didn't like it at all. I mulled over the mornings' events and decided to wait until the following Monday when I would be picked up at my home by the senior officer that initially interviewed me. He pulled up in front of my home in the car that the bank was providing for my business travels. During the ride to Glen Head I told him about my meeting with Moe the week before. He stared straight ahead and said, "Don't worry about him. Just do your job". That was easier said than done.

The first three months were spent getting used to a whole new lending culture, while enduring a lot of criticism from Moe. Finally I asked him right out if he would feel better if I resigned. His answer was a resounding "probably, because this just isn't going to work". In my eyes he was trying to discredit those that had hired me, by proving that they had made a huge mistake. I decided at that moment to prove him wrong. My work ethic and reputation started to pay off immediately as the referral stream started to bear some real fruit.

At the end of the first year I had exceeded every goal that had been set for me, but I always had the distinct feeling that Moe would bury me in a second if he had the opportunity. I never gave him the chance regardless of the number of times when he undermined my new business efforts, increased my annual goals to levels that were impossible to achieve, and if all of that didn't work he would come up with some new idea to make my life miserable. I never found out what his problem was, but over time I felt somewhat better when I realized that I wasn't alone. Each new hire was treated in much the same way.

CHAPTER FIFTEEN

In a small community bank you get to know everybody in a short span of time. My problems with my direct supervisor were overshadowed by the great respect I received from senior management, the lending officers and the branch personnel. I took great pride in telling everyone that I started literally at the bottom. It is my firm opinion that many of today's' bankers negate the importance of the branch staff. "What do they do anyway"? Take deposits, cash a few checks, and smile". The Teller is the first line of defense in any bank. They see most customers on a daily basis, and the lending officers or account officers only talk to these clients when there is a borrowing need or at loan renewal time.

During my forty three years working in the industry, I have heard thousands of comments from the biggest account relationships regarding the people that work in the branches. To the customer the branch is "my bank", and many a relationship was saved simply based upon the good relationship that a substantial customer had established with the branch staff. Senior management at First of Long Island understood the importance of teamwork like no other bank I had worked for. It was extremely difficult for the competition to steal a major account away because of this culture. It was common occurrence for an account officer to receive a call from the branch regarding a customer that may have commented about the slow turnaround on a loan request, a family illness, or a slowdown in his or her business. This information would provide valuable intelligence to the bank, and enable the account officer to act instead of having to react.

The information received would prompt a call of a visit to the customer, even if it was only to let them know that the bank appreciated their business, and we are always available when needed. I was visibly impressed when I witnessed senior management visit the branch offices, and stop by the teller stations to say hello and chat if only for a minute. In the early days of my career it wasn't that way, and most of the large banks failed to recognize anyone in the branch other than the manager. There was less competition back then, and not a priority to stress the importance of the entire team.

Government regulation of the banking industry had effectively caused the banks to eliminate individual lending authority, and constant visits by the "OCC" caused the banks to expand their loan review processes to ensure that all compliance guidelines were adhered to. First National Bank of Long Island had long endured a reputation as a bank that would be happy to lend money if in fact the borrower, didn't need any. The credit culture was indeed conservative, but this community bank wasn't often criticized by the regulatory agencies. It was consistently profitable, loan reserves and charge-offs were the lowest in the industry and they intended that they stay that way.

In 2005 a new president was brought in and the CEO retired soon after. I started to feel the effects of government regulations that literally made every decision a difficult one. All banks seemed to spend more time preparing for the next government audit or review than they would allocate to business development. I didn't enjoy going to work the way I used to, and criticism of the banking industry had only just begun. I had made myself a promise decades earlier to control my destiny and recognize the signals that would tell me it was time to get out. Near the end of 2005 those signals came in rapids succession. Make no mistake, I was not unhappy working at the First of Long Island. I was unhappy with what I perceived to be the direction that the industry was headed in.

I received the strongest signal to "get out", when a major client of mine had a bad year. This client was consistently profitable, but was in the construction business where the banks did not tolerate a bad year no matter how extenuating the circumstances might be. Fear of criticism by the regulatory agencies resulted in the bank calling the loan despite a totally understandable explanation for the loss, combined with a strong recommendation from the clients accounting firm. I defended my client to a point where I was reminded that I was employed by the bank, not the customer. Ultimately I assisted the client by introducing them to an associate at another bank. That client is still with that bank, and has been highly profitable since 2005. In my opinion it was fear of criticism that caused the bank to "shoot from the hip" and get out of the credit. It was easier than dealing with the scrutiny posed by the regulators. In fairness to the bank, it was also a very large borrowing relationship in a community bank, and would draw too much attention.

We were once again "deposit gatherers". The residential mortgage market was reaching a point of saturation, and the rumbling of a financial meltdown could be heard in the distance. The same government officials that had urged the banks to "loosen up", and find a way to provide one hundred percent financing for anyone that wanted it, were beginning to criticize the industry for liberal lending practices. It seemed that the only news that was being reported about the industry was bad news, and the securitization of mortgages was about to blow up under its own weight.

Then on an October day in 2006 I received a bit of bad news that would ultimately convince me to retire. I was asked to do some research at the Nassau County Clerk's office in Mineola and arrived there at nine o'clock when the office opened. The sign on the door also mandated that all cell phones be turned off before entering the building. I couldn't understand the reasoning but I complied. I requested the various files that I needed and found an available table and chair to work at. At noon I had some lunch at a local restaurant and returned to the clerk's office to finish up.

I remember looking at my watch at three thirty, and felt a nagging urge to check my phone for voice messages and missed calls. The project hadn't produced the results that we thought, so I returned the files and turned on the phone as I exited the lobby. As I stepped out into the sunlight the phone rang and it was my oldest daughter. I answered with my usual "Hi Honey, what's up"? Her voice immediately told me that something was very wrong.

"Dad, I just left the doctors' office. He told me that I have Cancer". I was stunned and felt helpless. What was I going to say to her? "Don't worry, everything will be fine"? I listened as she explained that the test results revealed that she has Internal Melanoma. She went on to tell me that she would have surgery at Sloan Kettering within a month. I found myself thinking, A Month? Why not tomorrow. I tried to soothe her concerns, but couldn't convince myself that she would be alright. I was still on the phone with her when I climbed into my car for the trip back to the office. We decided to talk again later that day and ended the call.

I called the office to check for messages, and told my secretary that I wouldn't be back that afternoon. I was quickly reminded that my supervisor had mandated that I return to the office each afternoon before heading home. It had been a common practice to head directly home after a late afternoon appointment, and not waste time and gas just to show your face back at the office for a few minutes. I was in no mood for this mercenary bullshit, and simply said, "He can do whatever he wants, but I am heading home".

CHAPTER SIXTEEN

As I stepped into the house my wife looked at my face and knew that bad news was coming. She immediately suspected that it was work related, and at that moment I wished that it was. I opened my mouth to speak and my emotions took over. Three words came out of my mouth, before I fell into her arms and lost it. "Dawn has Cancer". We spent the rest of that day talking with Dawn and other family members, reviewing the various surgical options that were suggested, and comforting her to the best of our ability.

I drove to our local church to pray and light some candles. I found myself negotiating with the Creator on my daughter's behalf. She was only in her thirties at the time, has a husband and an eight year old daughter. "Please give her more time, and take what you need from me". That night was a sleepless night, the first of many when I stared at the ceiling in the darkness searching for answers. I had an uncanny ability to solve problems in my personal life and in my career, but now I felt helpless, a feeling that I wasn't used to, and didn't like at all.

The next morning I literally forced myself into the shower, got dressed and drove to the office. I fully expected to be reprimanded for my actions the previous day and I wasn't wrong. Moe looked angry and I went on the offense before he could say a word. "I received a call from my daughter around four thirty to tell me she was diagnosed with Internal Melanoma. Do what you must, but she is my first priority right now". I turned and walked to my desk without waiting for his reply. Several hours later he approached me and asked if there was anything that he could do to help. He was a cancer survivor and understood the pain of the entire nightmare. I thanked him and told him that I would keep him in the loop, but would do what I must going forward.

One month later Dawn checked into Sloan for surgery, and it went well, but the surgeon wasn't immediately optimistic about the prognosis going forward. He felt that he got it all but internal melanoma is referred to as the "hiding cancer" that could erupt anywhere in the body without warning. She would undergo a catalog of tests every few months for a very long time. The first round were clean and we as a family would breathe easy for a few months until it was time for the next round. We would wait for the phone to ring with the results and repeat that process over and over again.

Going to work each day would give me a brief respite from the constant worry, but it was no longer fun to be banker. We would spend more time dealing with regulatory requirements and our customers would suffer long delays waiting for a decision when financing was required. We all knew that bankers wore "belts and suspenders" when making credit decisions, but now we were also stapling our trousers to our bodies to reduce or eliminate any risk. Blaming the process on the regulators was no consolation to a client that needed a prompt decision.

It was mid-December of 2005 when I advised the bank that I would retire at the end of April the following year. I faced the usual questions about my decision to retire at a time when my thinking may not be clear, but my mind was made up. I knew that I would have to earn for a few more years, but at that point I needed to remove one level of stress from my life, and that was banking. I had never been unemployed for a single day during a career that spanned forty three years, something that I was very proud of. No one would pat me on the shoulder and ask me to leave the office immediately when the banks decided to down size, reorganize, right size or "purge", one of my favorites. I watched far too many associates fall apart when their careers were abruptly terminated without any reason or advanced warning.

One such incident that has stayed with me occurred in 1995 when one of the Money Center banks needed to downsize after several rapid fire mergers. I was out on calls one Monday morning and returned to my office in Melville shortly before noon. I noticed small groups of people talking in whispers, and looking left and right as they spoke. The mood was somber and the conversation was extremely serious. I approached one such group and casually asked, "What's going on"? I was updated in a matter of seconds, by the group that kept looking over one shoulder and then the other. They were frightened, and I quickly began to understand why.

Early that morning a "raiding party" of senior officers walked through the office, and advised some of the personnel to step away from what they were doing, take their personal belongings and follow them outside the building where they were advised that they had been terminated. They were told to go home and await further instructions from Human Resources. If an individual had the use of a bank owned automobile, they had to surrender the keys and make other arrangements to get home. Those that had a cell phone called a relative or friend to pick them up, and others just stood in the old morning air with stunned looks on their faces. No reason was offered for the terminations, and questions were not answered. They were told that any effort to re-enter the building would be regarded as trespassing.

The people that were let go that day were without exception, long term loyal employees that had no history of problems. I guess it was just time to clean out the higher paid individuals and replace them at some future time with younger, less expensive employees. No one was admitting to that process, and it was just termed, "job elimination". The days of my youth when I was told to come in on time, do a good days work and enjoy job security were certainly over. Within a few hours the projects that these individuals were working on were gathered up and disseminated to other people for completion. No one was complaining about a heavy workload after what had happened. Those that remained were just happy to have a job, and they worked like robots for many months. I guess that management had achieved several goals that morning. Several weeks later, the senior officer who was assigned the task of carrying out the deed was also terminated without warning.

I never forgot this chain of events and made a promise to recognize the signs and listen to "my gut". In December of 2005 I advised the bank that I would retire at the end of April 2006.

CHAPTER SEVENTEEN

I spent the last five months of my banking career occupying an empty desk at the Trust department in Woodbury and was transferred one last time to the Regional Lending office in Hauppauge where I reported to a senior officer that I had trained many years before. He treated me well, and pretty much left me alone during the final two months. He remembered all too well, that I had taken an interest in him twenty years earlier and he still had fond memories of those days. I had given him the best piece of advice that I had received so many years ago while working at Bankers Trust Company. "Watch how you treat people on your way up, because you never know who you will run into on your way down". Those words had come full circle, and the message rang true. That's why I've repeated the phrase a number of times during this writing.

My final day was April 28th, 2006. I drove the bank owned car to the main office in Glen Head, signed some documents in Human Resources, had one last lunch with a few close friends, and said my final goodbye's. At 4PM I exited the building and waited in the parking lot for my ride home. John Solensky arrived a few minutes later and I climbed into the passenger seat and buckled up for the fifteen mile trip from Glen Head to north Wantagh. I was able to take in the scenic trip through Upper Brookville past the equestrian centers, golf courses and residential estates that adorned both sides of route 106, also named Cedar Swamp Road. John was quiet, and allowed me to record that final mental picture of a daily commute that started almost ten years earlier. When we finally crossed under Jericho Turnpike and drove past the first of many shopping malls I turned my head in his direction and spoke the first words of the trip.

"Let's keep in touch and get together for lunch once in a while." John agreed, but deep inside I guess I knew that those long term work relationships very often die off quickly. The common bonds that are built working in the same office, the daily trials and tribulations of working in an industry that has endured so many major changes would be gone for me at least, and John would have to endure a bit longer. Eight years later I can state that our friendship has remained intact, and has grown stronger. Our lunch meetings when I am very often looking at the Quick Draw lottery screen at a local pub allow us to discuss the latest changes in the banking industry, launch our verbal attack on the regulators, and discuss simpler times. The good old days were just that, but bankers are now regarded as one level beneath the legal profession.

Our government continues to portray our proud industry as tools of the rich. The left has found a successful way to turn the 90% against the 10% that have accumulated all the wealth, despite the fact that this same group created and maintains tens of millions of jobs. The liberal faction is focused on an "UNFAIR" distribution of wealth, and the promise to remedy this situation has resulted in election mandates throughout the country. We are headed in a direction that could evolve into pure socialism, regardless of the fact that it has failed throughout the rest of our world. Only time will tell if the general population becomes disillusioned with empty campaign promises that result in zero change

CHAPTER EIGHTEEN
A Second Career.

During the first month of my "retirement" I kept busy doing all of the long put off projects around the house, complete with the spring planting of flowers and a vegetable garden. Each morning I would sit at the kitchen table with a cup of coffee and watch the "lemmings" leave for work. The same people pass by each morning and return each evening looking drained and exhausted. Despite the fact that the daily pressure was now behind me, I often had the feeling that I needed to be someplace else, but that feeling quickly subsided. Jan and I had planned a family vacation to celebrate my retirement and we left for Paradise Island on June 4th for a five day celebration. Several of our children, their spouses and four grandchildren met us at Kennedy Airport for the early morning flight. We paid all the bills during that trip, except for personal gambling and alcohol consumption. The only rule required that we met as a family for dinner each day. We had a ball and returned home with memories that will last a lifetime.

Two weeks after our return the phone rang around eight thirty on a

Monday morning. "Too early for family or friends to be calling." I started to worry about my mother who was ninety two at the time and still functioning on her own in a small condo in New Jersey. My fears were quickly allayed when I heard the voice of an accountant that I had worked with over the past twenty years. After some small talk about my soon to be "short lived" retirement he asked if I might be interested in a consulting relationship with his firm. I always knew that I would need to earn for several years, but I asked if I could think about it get back to him. Within several days I called him and suggested that we meet for breakfast. We agreed to meet the following day at the Carle Place Diner. I mentioned that I had a golf date at eleven and was assured that we would need an hour at most.

The next morning I dressed in golf slacks and shirt and drove to the diner. The person I had spoken with was already seated at a table waiting for me, and was accompanied by the Managing Partner of the firm. I also knew him well, and our breakfast was interrupted many times by well-wishers from the business and banking community that I had dealt with during my 43 year career. Several of these people would become consulting clients of mine during the next eight years. In less than an hour we had hammered out a consulting agreement where I would perform as an advocate of the firm, and hopefully help them generate new clients. The managing partner would need to discuss the matter with his executive committee at the next meeting in several weeks and would get back to me.

As I drove to the golf course I realized that my golf bag was in the trunk of my other car. I made a quick trip back home to pick them up. My wife was standing on the front porch talking on the phone. I heard her say, "here he is, I'll put him on." The managing partner had polled the executive committee by phone and our deal was approved. Within a week I formed a corporation and started to build a consulting practice. The word got around quickly and within a few months I had attracted other clients in a variety of businesses. The accounting firm asked me to assist clients that needed some sort of financing in addition to the business development responsibilities. I also noticed very quickly that most of those clients required construction finance and permanent mortgages on their new or existing business premises. 2006 was not a good time to ask any bank to provide anything other than a short term line of credit or a term loan to finance equipment purchases.

I would qualify each need for financing and attempt to match the client with the right bank, review the financial statements and move the process forward. As a retired banker I was looked upon as an individual that would never waste time trying to force feed a marginal deal to any bank. The fact that all deals appeared to be marginal at a time when the banking system was in poor shape resulted in tons of frustration for me and my clients. For the first time I actually knew what the business community had to endure. "I've been in business over thirty years, make money each year, and lived up to all my prior commitments to my bank. Why can't they get this deal done for me, Ed?" I heard the same reasons over and over again. "We used to do that stuff all the time, but not in this environment."

One of my clients built, owns and manages several major flag hotels. He has successfully completed each project well within budget and on time, but was faced with a myriad of reasons to decline any request for financing regardless of the superb track record. The Hospitality industry which includes hotels and restaurants was hit very hard in the last economic downturn, and no banker wanted to face the obvious questions from the regulators. "Didn't you guys learn anything during the past five years?" Despite all the assurances that I received from my core of friendly bankers, each attempt to obtain financing took forever, and the deal seemed to change over time and become more difficult for me and my client to swallow. More than once I was asked to withdraw the loan request when the client became frustrated at the conditions and covenants that resulted each time the underwriters reviewed the deal. It quickly became apparent that no client deserved to go through this exhausting process, and that no client could pay me enough to endure the pain along with them. But I did.

Another client was in the construction business, focusing on Municipal and Public Works projects. "Another tough industry for us to finance Ed." The client provides construction services for various government agencies, and we all know how that works. They can withhold payment at any time for any reason, and the bank is unwilling to assume that risk. Another example of different standards for different people. Let any tax payer withhold payment for any reason and that person will incur all the wrath and fury that the government can muster. Government agencies can pretty much do whatever they want, because they really can't be held liable for damages etc. They never seem to pay a price for their mistakes.

CHAPTER NINETEEN

I was now working two or three days a week, but to hear my wife talk about my new "part time career", I was on the phone or on the computer day and night, even on the weekends. She was right, and I was now working more hours than I did as a banker. On the other hand, I never wanted to become the annoying, pain in the ass retiree that I heard so many talk about. When I wasn't working on a specific deal, I kept busy in other ways. I've enjoyed a long term membership in the Long Island Business Development Council on Long Island. This group supports business owners looking to grow and expand. The membership includes most, if not all of the banks, Small Business Administration, accounting firms, builders, developers, brokers, the various Industrial Development agencies that operate on Long Island, and the list goes on. It continues to be a valuable forum for business owners, and certainly allows me to keep my fingers on the pulse of the local banking scene.

As a career bankers I found it frustrating when any client or prospective client would shop his or her deal to several banks. It usually led to a bidding war, and also questioned the client's loyalty. I would interview several banks and discuss the merits of each bank with the client. We would invite the favored bank to visit with us, lay out the deal along with a list of so called "deal breakers", conditions or covenants that the client would not accept. Too many times we were told that the bank would proceed along those lines, and months later we would receive a Term Sheet or Commitment Letter containing the deal breakers that we discussed on day one. I guess we put all of our eggs in one basket, only to find them scrambled at a later date. So much for doing the right thing. I can now understand why a business owner would want to shop his deal.

In the 1960s a handshake was a commitment. Today it represents nothing more than a mechanism to buy some time. The banker meeting with my client must take the deal to higher ground where it is analyzed and scrutinized by people that hadn't developed a relationship with the client. The analyst or credit officer didn't meet with us and develop a gut feeling regarding the project to be financed or the people that would stand behind it. They are only concerned about securing the banks position, and satisfying the regulators that are always there to criticize. As a result the banker feels the need to remove any hint of risk in any loan. In my era we always referred to "risk reward" which ultimately led to analysis of risk, term and purpose. Ultimately a deal was priced accordingly because bankers were business people and were entitled to a reasonable return on each deal. And "yes", some deals ultimately went bad. That's the risk you take in any business, even the business of government, where laws are enacted without thorough analysis of the negative effects. One recent example is Obamacare, where the negative effects far outweigh the positive intentions. This is of course my opinion, but then again this is my friggin book.

Who in government pays a price for bad legislation? Who gets jail time or pays huge fines? No one, but the long term damage ultimately always falls on the taxpayer. Elected officials are never expected to be perfect. They are only human. Their mistakes are always justified as a result of trying to fix some social issue, and concern for the rest of the population isn't a priority. We have the power to do something about this double standard, but we parse our words, and tone down our anger, lest we release the beast that is only known as "the regulators." WE HAVE THE POWER TO CHANGE THINGS. It certainly won't be easy or quick, but it can be done. Read on my friends.

CHAPTER TWENTY

The best tool to effect change is education. Our government has learned that constant criticism of big business works all too well at the polls. The poor, minority groups and the female vote have become the focus of their lies and rhetoric. The labor unions have also rallied behind the promises of positive change for the average family that does nothing but struggle to get by, while the rich continue to get richer at their expense. "It's time to spread it around" became a rallying cry that appealed to most voters. Entitlements have become a way of life for several generations, and the will to work among some citizens has been blurred by the availability of social programs that are just too easy to access. As a result the far left benefited from a significant electoral mandate. By the way, Social Security isn't an entitlement. Each of us paid into the fund all of our working lives, while the politicians raided it for other programs. Shouldn't some of them go to jail for that?

The end result has been a slowdown in business, elimination of jobs, massive unemployment and battles on Capitol Hill that in the end has achieved little for our country or its people. Our representatives in government have little or no business experience, and risk is something that only the "wrongdoers", the rich flirt with. We see our country traveling down a path towards total socialism, and we all know how that has worked in the past. We also see hundreds of billions of "tax payer dollars" going to foreign aid. Many of those countries have no problem taking our money and even less of a problem taking our lives. Who are we to force our ideology on others? Well, "they want to live like we do, don't they?" The real truth is that they don't but we keep on investing our taxpayer dollars in one failure after another. Who pays the price for those failures? Certainly not the politicians. "Well, we tried to bring democracy to these countries, but it just didn't work".

Those same politicians have no problem going after big business and have the Balls to tell our citizens that tax payer dollars will be used to bail them out. What a bunch of hypocrites. Billions that have been squandered on "piss poor" foreign aid could effectively pay for higher education and health care for every man woman and child in this country. And yet these unqualified people continue to win elections, and ultimately make more bad decisions. It's time to turn this ship around.

Big business has the ability to implement change by looking within its own ranks for viable candidates who cannot only talk the talk, but have walked the walk. Most of them started with an idea and very little money. They worked tirelessly, hired the brightest people who also possessed a strong work ethic and built their businesses. They also know how to create and implement a budget, something that is completely foreign to government.

The banks were always there to finance the growth and expansion, which ultimately created jobs and benefits for the employees. Those loans were repaid and many of those businesses became public companies. The stockholders thought it wise to invest in them and in most cases profited from those investments. Businesses started by small people who became financial giants that are now cast in a negative tone as "the rich".

Big business needs to tell their story to every employee, customer and investor. Who among them could have succeeded without the banks? It took a generation for things to get this bad, and it will take another to make it right. The banks and big business also need to go on the attack. The need to communicate has never been more important than it is now. I've successfully counseled my clients on the negative role of government in business, and the effect it has on getting deals done when financing is required. Every banker should counsel their clients in the same manner, even if it only helps them achieve a higher level of patience in enduring the process. Place the blame where it belongs and over time the information will trickle down and make sense to more people. Support the right candidates and get them elected. My sentiments are shared by an increasing number of bankers. Our industry has been victimized for too long.

I recently organized an economic development event on Long Island, and our featured speaker was a former CEO of a regional bank that was absorbed in a merger with a larger institution. He talked about the effects of government regulation and shared some startling information. "Five years ago I ran a sixteen billion dollar bank and was able to staff the risk management and compliance department with twenty three people. I now run a 1.6 billion dollar bank and employ over 130 people in risk management and compliance at a cost that exceeds five million dollars a year." With more regulation of our financial institutions on the horizon, it becomes clear that more time, money and energy will be dedicated to adhering to regulation in the next five years. "It's time to endorse the right candidates, and support them at the polls. We need a change, and we need it now."

As I listened to his comments, I thought of simpler times, and longed for their return. The trip back begins in the voting booths.

FIN